LOOSE WINE

Also by J:C:MACK

The Last Siesta

LOOSE WINE

A Story of Sfuso - Italian Table Wine

J:C:MACK

INGRESSO BOOKS

First edition 2015

LOOSE WINE/J:C:MACK
ISBN-13:978-1495972409
10:1495972402

INGRESSO BOOKS
J:C:MACK
Literary information: info@ingressobooks.com

Photo Credits: p.92, p.145, F.J.McAvoy.
All other illustrations, archival material.

To my good friend Salvatore, and all those diligent and unsung Italian viticulturists.

Table of Contents

Preface

I A Foot in the Door: 1
II Actors and Spectators: 5
III Concrete and Wood: 12
IV A Question of Identity: 18
V From the Beginning: 25
VI Genesis. Birth of a Vineyard: 36
VII A Mixed Case of Agronomics: 46
VIII Ad Infinitum: 53
IX A sense of Order: 65
X To Be or Not to Be: 70
XI Dionysian Harvest: 83
XII Pranzo: 94
XIII In the Lap of the Gods: 102
XIV Sugar: 117
XV A Question of Taste: 122
XVI Back to the Beginning: 130
XVII Vino della Casa: 133

The Novice's Lament: 151

Glossary
Appendix
Further reading
Index

List of Illustrations

Chianini. 8
Podere vats.16
Enoteca: Galluzzo, Florence. 23
Abandoned farmhouse: ad hoc annexes. 29
Fiat bulldozer. 40
Primi Pali. 42
Cartoccio. 44
Pali with cross-poles. 48
Tuscan vineyard. 52
Trained branches. 60
Grappolo. 67
Malvasia grapes. 70
54 litre Demijohns. 82
Vendemmia - Grape picking. 87
Plastic crates. 88
Diraspatrice. 90
Torchio. Ancient wooden grape press. 92
Bollitore. 100
Vinaccia. 106
Strettoio. 107
Compressed *vinaccia.* 116
Fibreglass vat. 123
Demijohn with *Bollitore.* 124
Wine containers. 133
Cork stopper. 134
Erba Vetriola in bottles. 136
Tiraolio. 140
Stoppa. 141
Gomma del vino. 143
Schiuma. 145
Bigoncia and *Frollatura.* 148
Vineyard battalions. 149
Buying direct. 149

"The vine, which is to be the companion of man, is waywardly docile in its growth, falling into festoons beside his cornfields, or roofing his garden walks, or casting the shadows all summer upon his door."

John Ruskin: Modern Painters.

PREFACE

Those reading this book may be surprised to find that humbler wines, perhaps not rising to any great merit, still share a lineal ancestry with the noblest of their kind.

Therefore, its sole purpose is to familiarize the reader not with fine wines, of which there are many excellent books, but with the universal method of production suited to the everyday need for wine by the citizen in Italy, and Tuscany in particular.

It is an ancient story, many thousands of years in the making, but fundamentally only marginally different today than of old. But there have been changes, mostly the result of agricultural technology, and as always these advances effect a way of life, especially for the people who work on the land.

In truth, we are at a point where the old pattern of farming is on the cusp of extinction, and especially in the making of wine. To describe this account in a meaningful way necessitates placing it in a social and agrarian context, and it seemed that the best way to do that was to experience such an activity first hand before the inevitable advances obscured it altogether. In this it became a personal narrative. At the same time I have taken the liberty to augment the experience with those historical and anecdotal aspects which seem to have influenced the development of viticulture, lost as so many of them have been by time and indifference. These rather 'pepper' the pages, but I trust will helpfully amplify the context.

The book then, is not a criticism of change, only a reflection on what will change.

Initially, the transformation that took place in European agriculture began in the United Kingdom with the first 'Enclosures Act' of 1773 that profoundly altered society, making possible the sustained growth of population, and the 'Industrial Revolution'. The same effect spread throughout Europe at a slower pace, and became relevant in Italy by the massive social revolution inspired by the *'Riforma Agraria'*, given its first proposed framework by Benito Mussolini who contemplated the compulsory acquisition of estates, and transformation of tenants into proprietors. A post-war democratic government finally chose to instigate the enactment of such a policy. Few in Italy at the time really understood what momentous changes would take place, stubbornly believing that the farm worker, or *contadino,* would be at liberty to continue their former way of life unchanged. However, change, like time, waits for no man!

Demographic forces, education, industrial expansion and smaller families made the sustaining of such an agricultural life too precarious for these farms, and emigration from the land became the only solution.

The remnants of these small working units remain today mostly in the hands of an older generation born at the onset of the Second World War. Their sons and daughters - if still on the land - have embraced technology, and a completely new business ethic. The old life, still dimly reflected in the new, will soon be a faint echo only discernable to social historians.

One of those echoes is the ubiquitous making of wine. Not grand vintages for the sophisticated ruminations of city dinner parties, or the intellectual analysis of the discerning critic, but of an everyday wine for family meal times. *Contadini* or *citadini,* it matters little, for they all come from the same soil that is Italy, and the tradition of *Vino Locale* is common to them all.

The title of the book, 'Loose Wine', (*Sfuso*) may sound rather eccentric, and to be truthful, is so colloquial in Italy that one would be hard pressed to discover a meaningful definition of the phrase in print. Standard dictionaries generally only include wine as another example under '*Sfuso*', and leave the rest to your imagination. Therefore, I'll attempt a fuller explanation.

The term '*sfuso*' has its root in the classical Latin '*effusus*', corrupted into its vulgar form, '*exfusus*' - to pour out. The English word 'effuse' is derived from it, meaning to pour forth, unrestrained.

In modern Italian '*sfuso*' means offered loose; that is, supplied loose rather than as a standard packaged measure. It suggests that it will be poured, or received in this way, even if it will eventually be in a container of some sort. As such, you can purchase various fruits and vegetables in this manner during the season, though they may also be typically described as '*sciolto*' in some shops. Wine sold from a bulk vessel, very often a vat, into a container supplied by the purchaser, is generally referred to as *sfuso.* Though perhaps only a quota of the same year's wine that commercially may be destined for barrel ageing, *sfuso* is selected, and set aside in the cantina, for earlier consumption.

***Sfuso*, as a term, does not in any way imply a standard, or quality. It is a method of supplying wine, and as such, used in the text, denotes no more than a wine offered in this way.**

The references to *sfuso* are referring to a young wine that is in the making, or ready for drinking. And that is all. For those who like it very young this may be as early as four months from the harvest.

Sfuso must not be confused with *'Vino Novello'*, a commercially bottled wine for which a premium has to be paid. For *Vino Novello* the grapes are allowed to ferment whole before being crushed and placed in vats for the second fermentation. No additional yeast is added, and the wine cannot be sold before the beginning of November in the year of its *vendemmia*.

There is a tendency to dismiss any consideration between what is essentially a 'farm wine' and an 'estate wine'. The latter phrase is coined here to indicate wine that has been aged, in wood. It is well to consider the fundamental difference between the two, and while there is no such argument for an Italian, it is probably politic in the circumstances, to explain the practical distinction for those who wish to immerse themselves in rural Italy. By the end of this book the reader should find themselves suitably enlightened.

After all, no one would draw a parallel between a potato and a pomegranate though they are both edible. Equally, no one should between *sfuso* and fine wine. All wine is naturally dependent on the grape, but its function thereafter is quite divergent, and its utilization a matter of etiquette. Therefore, *sfuso* needs to be approached with a totally different 'mind set'.

I have appended a glossary to accompany that elusive term that may have been explained previously but is not easily brought to mind. One or two, being of a colloquial nature, invariably defy a standard Italian/English lexicon, and the reader may, if they wish, spend a few fruitful hours trying to make head or tail of them - accompanied by a glass or two of wine, of course.

J:C:MACK. 2015

I: A Foot in the Door

In the beginning there's always a touch of motivation. Sometimes it's ambition. In my case it was an accident.

I sat forking and twirling my way through a *Penne all'arrabbiata*, hoping eating alone wouldn't become a habit. The *trattoria* wasn't busy, so without company I eavesdropped on a foursome opposite.

Tuscany in summer is full of small groups hell bent on discovering what all the magic is about. Smart Italian restaurants they can find in any urban high street, and in the words of that knowledgeable travel writer, H.V.Morton: 'As the best wine in Italy is rarely found in a bottle, so the best cooking is often enjoyed in a cellar or a room that contains no more than ten tables.'

Therefore, you need to be of an inquisitive bent.

For something authentic the intrepid venture into the dusty alleyways of medieval lanes, looking for a place full of loquacious locals where the menu outside is described in the vernacular. I'd been the same after all. Tourists like the squad on the table next to me: inquisitive, smart enough not to be pretentious in knowing what *Polpette alla pizzaiola* is. Angelo, the waiter, animatedly scraped the bottom of his rudimentary English, stabbing at their proffered help. That was it. "Four of those - *per favore*."

He left them with the wine list. It wasn't extensive,

consisting of only two types: "Must be rubbish at that price," and "As long as you're paying!" Compromising, they settled for the house wine that sometimes doesn't even appear on the bill, which says a great deal for the fiscal responsibility of the *padrone*. God bless him.

"Good?" they asked.

"*Benissimo*," Angelo said enthusiastically. "*Il vino locale. Sfuso.*"

I don't know if they enjoyed their *Polpette*, and I certainly don't know if they understood the meaning of the term *sfuso* in respect of the local wine, but they spent a lot of time discussing the contents of the ceramic jug festooned with purple grapes and verdant foliage that had been set between them. It must have been giving their analytical taste buds a hard time, because they ordered another to be on the safe side.

One thing; however, stuck in my mind. They had come to the conclusion that it was better than the house wine they'd sampled the night before.

Now there's a thing - was one table wine really that different from another? Had I been overlooking something? They certainly weren't talking *grand crus*, even if they were talking in Burgundian style of thousands of tiny vineyards of a very small acreage. Neither were they talking about the sublime skills of a shipper's cellar-master. They were talking about the local *sfuso*, wine no one talked about. It was just there. At noon and evening. On the table, along with the water.

After fifteen years mooching about my little bit of Tuscany, with frequent trips up and down the rest of the peninsula, I realized from their conversation that I hadn't been very perceptive, or even inquisitive, about the wine I was consuming. I'd just, quite happily, taken it for granted.

I stared interrogatively into the glass in front of me for some half expected inspiration. It wasn't one of those Brandy Balloon size glasses that take up so much room on the table there's little left for the cruets and castors, but a squat, thick glass tumbler, redolent of any authentic *trattoria*. This distinction alone told me something was different. I wasn't drinking a noble wine on my modest resources, but it struck me that there was still an awful lot of variation in the 'red stuff', even at the accepted mundane level I was in the habit of frequenting. Acknowledging that they were heterogeneous; being created from different grapes in different regions, I realized I was also considering a concept; an abstract idea. Wine writers it appears, don't like abstract ideas. They are used to having an appellation. Bottles are required to possess a label. Clues that can identify a whole lot of prejudices or, conversely, prime those experienced taste buds in what to expect, and what to judge. After all, who'd buy a bottle of wine without a label?

Somewhat surprisingly, millions of Italians do.

So I made a few enquiries, and someone pointed me in the direction of someone else, who introduced me to someone who made *vino della casa,* which is the same as *vino da tavola,* which is that *vino locale, sfuso.*

Of the three, I suppose *vino locale* might more accurately describe the subject that appears in the following pages. Therefore, simply assume it means a wine destined to remain in its provincial setting, though restaurants will travel considerable distances if they consider a particular wine is worthwhile. It then becomes more aptly, *vino della casa.*

In the event, the man I met turned out to be a familiar face, having noticed his considerable presence before, at one opera or another; someone who expressed himself generously with a great deal of kinetic energy, vocally demonstrating his appreciation for the artiste if they had favoured us with an agreeable rendering of an aria. That of course, might strike an opera buff as nothing out of the ordinary, bearing in mind that an Italian audience always has a predilection for signalling its admiration of a good performance, or its declamation if it's bad! The *loggioniste* of the world famous 'La Scala' opera house in Milan, are renowned for their unruly behaviour.

Well, without the slightest doubt you'd recognize him as a distinctively Italian enthusiast, and which in the circumstances, proved a good enough reason for me to meet Lorenzo Benini.

When he'd stopped chuckling, and considered if I was being serious, he nodded, and suggested expansively, "All right. If you're so interested, there's plenty of time until the next *vendemmia.* In the New Year we'll make a start. Meanwhile, you can come along and help me if you can spare the time. *Va bene*?"

Perhaps he meant to humour me; perhaps he just displayed with notable Italian patience, a respect for a foreigner's dream; or perhaps he'd become fed up with being on his own among the vines.

Whatever it was, no one mentioned that - in what can only be described as entering a historical time capsule - I'd find myself taking part in the sort of husbandry that will soon be long past, and which in reality, is already half gone.

That's how it came about: this story of a wine that has no label, and to the consternation of many, doesn't even have a proper name.

Lorenzo Benini is a large man. Not an archetypal Italian to be sure - rather one you'd expect to find among the incense, towering marble naves, and maternal Madonnas of some great Tuscan church. You might also be forgiven, and he will surely forgive you, in imagining that he is the specious manifestation of a well-fed, gregarious cardinal. Rosy cheeks lifted into beaming smiles, stentorian voice, a generous manner, and an enthusiasm for that expressive style of life that ended with Pope Innocent IX.

If he could have been a man for the epicurean passions of the Renaissance world, today you must seek him elsewhere. And passions he has. For grand Italian opera in which he is an erudite and amusing savant; and because - being the lotion and potion for all ills as Donizetti's Dr. Dulcamara would have us believe - he expends a fair portion of this ardour on the making of wine.

You will, assuredly, search in vain for a label designating his product, nor find a single bottle among the serried ranks displayed in the countless designer *enoteche* that have sprung up in practically every Tuscan town. This is not an omission, or an indication that Italians in any shape or form, view the long arm of the fiscal authorities in the same way as others view the grim reaper; nor that they practice anonymity as a sleight - of - hand to avoid the distinction of familiarity or notoriety in matters of finance.

There is a very simple and practical reason why their absence might seem to resemble some dark secret, and it is not because they are shy in making an appearance.

Profit in this arcane world of *sfuso* can be - invariably is - almost accidental when their production is often so erratic, let alone in such minimalist quantities. With sometimes only half a hectare (one and a quarter acres) of vines under cultivation they're not actually going to be so awash with wine as to contemplate the need for wellington boots, and a yearly audit. Production for them is not something for which they are likely to require the assistance of a market.

Unsurprisingly, there are more substantial farms whose proprietors had found it profitable to increase their vineyard acreage, and supply those legendary

Italian hostelries, the local *osterie* and *trattorie*, as well as the small city *cantine* catering for the local citizen. Nevertheless, to achieve this they will as likely use those time-honoured methods that closely parallel the semi - domestic rural producer providing for an immediate family.

Though clearly a question of magnitude, there's little difference in the degree of effort required to produce a given quantity of grapes on a small farm or a larger one. It's merely a question of multiplicity and professionalism. As in ancient times, it pays to settle for a larger family!

Apparently, only the *stranieri* from any number of foreign countries can sit under the umbrella pines, glass in hand, and dream the dream. Others have to stretch a leg among the vines for their benefit.

That then, in a nutshell, is the essence of Benini's labour. He makes wine for himself, his family, and for those lucky enough to be counted among his friends.

It's an esoteric and timeless product of the Italian countryside, like *Nipatella*, a wild aromatic herb that could be a substitute for everything; or the ever more elusive *Trombetta da Morto,* an equally wild, violet-black, edible mushroom that refuses to be a substitute for anything. That they are both representative of a European species is not likely to be something that will galvanize anyone into sending out search parties to find them among the sadly, much depleted British woodlands.

But in Tuscany, where trespassing laws are limited, and forests plentiful, you still come across such provisions for the country kitchen being collected and used as they were in times long past. That is, in much the same way as they treat another ancient staple of the countryside, *sfuso*. The bucolic way of life has not gone 'the way of all things', just yet.

For that reason, Benini seems in absolutely no hurry to keep up with the modern millennium Joneses. Why would he? He likes the natural, honest life of those venerable country farmers: open spaces, clean air, and the friendship of the soil. Besides, anyone would find it difficult making wine on a Tuscan farm sitting in a bank, fiddling with a carburettor in a garage, or taking a patient's blood pressure in a surgery. The truth is, part time is no time in the life of a grape. There has to be a consistency, a measured rhythm keeping time with nature, and the propagation of plants. You have to dedicate a great deal of energy if you're to manage them both successfully. There are some brave souls who do, but the circumstances have to be unique, and aren't open to all.

Not that Benini considers himself unique in this scheme of things. No one could mistake him for an antiquated farming fossil working from dawn to dusk. He too has other things to occupy his time. Therefore, he still has a need to rely on one other alternative, that of his own energetic factotum helping keep things in harmony with the persistent seasonal demands of viticulture.

Nilo Bacci, who has been associated with the farm since time immemorial, seems to know every vine and tuft of grass on the land by name. They are all conveniently called *lui,* which sounds like a proper noun in English, but in Italian is the third person singular, meaning nothing more familiar than 'him'.

When the mood takes Nilo, he will demonstrate that the impromptu classical amusement of the *'Canti Estemporanei'* still lives on. Though originally it took the form of a rhyming contest with two participants, and was decidedly off the cuff, nowadays it more often takes the form of *vers libre,* or a ballad. Nevertheless, they are still prodigiously long compositions on a Homeric scale, taken out and dusted down during the harvest.

Though he responds happily to the name Nilo he has another, a sobriquet, that nearly all Tuscan youths acquire, and which very often remains an appendage into maturity. However, as they are often descriptive, its continued existence is probably not always quite so welcome. His friends jocularly call him *Tappino,* meaning little cork in deference to his small size, while Benini, given his robust stature, answers to *Grandone* that in terms of size and character seems particularly apt.

Nilo, like so many of the classical farming community, is an essential Jack-of-all-trades. He is as happy bringing joy to the plumbing, as he is lying under a tractor that has been accused of making peculiar mechanical noises, or decanting puddles of dirty oil every time it stops. Whether such machines are treated with the same reverence as those now almost forgotten and deified creatures, the gently swaying white oxen of Chianti and the Maremma, it is difficult to say, but their character and tireless capacity seems to have a great deal in common.

Chianini.

In the manner of all farming gentlemen the pair seem only too eager to argue over everything, mostly it appears on nothing more prosaic than the opportunity to banter over incidents that have long since passed into history, and can thus be resurrected and embroidered to create a fresh angle on an old and half remembered event. Yet between them, by some miracle of temperament, they manage to sustain a precarious tempo in the production of wine.

This at first seems doubtful; given the tricks and spoofs they not only play on each other - but also anyone else who happen to be handy. You soon learn to keep a wary eye on their movements when one of them asks you to turn on the tap, in case you find the end of the hose discreetly tucked in your pocket!

In this they are both representative of a once ubiquitous, but now almost unique, Italian fraternal society - exhibited, as one would expect, by a presence that is exclusively male. They are each a true *terrae filius*, those inestimable sons of the earth. Any innocent bystander can only suppose that their feminine counterparts are all discreet and sensible ladies now!

Where *sfuso* is concerned, countless little farms throughout the length and breadth of Italy are probably happily, and busily, experiencing exactly the same thing. Those fabulous wine lakes that once appeared flooding the lines of journalistic hyperbole, if not the glasses of inebriates, turned out to exist only in the sums of Brussels bureaucrats; a figment seemingly created to support the passing of purely ornamental laws. Conceivably, no one saw fit to inform them that if the taxes on wine had been rationalized, and the market left to find its own equilibrium, then those imagined problems wouldn't exist! The pious will still say that at least the figurative dam hasn't been breached.

Be as that may, the author Burton Anderson at some recent point, established that there are 1.5 million registered vineyards in Italy, and that only 0.25% of the 7 billion litres of wine produced is exported.

That suggests that the bulk of the wine produced on these minuscule estates, often no more than very substantial gardens, along with the large commercial vineyards, is all consumed locally at an orthodox epicurean hour - An English breakfast being considered unorthodox, even to a late night Italian gastronome!

As mentioned earlier, a number of commercial vineyards, perhaps conscious that ambience and quality are more important to them than actual acres in production, also seem content to subscribe to this tradition. Only the choicest grapes will find their way into the mercantile product of their genius - and in the fullness of time, having spent a period maturing in casks, and another interval in bottles, may be given that impressive à la mode sticky label proclaiming them as a *Riserva*.

The remaining surplus is far from superfluous, being either presented mainly as a standard 0.75 litre bottle of some stated origin or, having perhaps been nothing more generous than a few kilos too many in the scheme of things, will have found itself swiftly set aside to provide *sfuso* for early, if not quite instant, consumption.

The economics of commerce responding to the dynamics of finance and fashion, don't always appear entirely rational. No one would consider this an ethical question, even if rather more questionably, a legal one. Under Italian law, those wines carrying the DOC or DOCG label of quality have, among other specification, their production regulated by *hectolitres* per hectare. (It doesn't necessarily guarantee a superior wine, only that the wine conforms to the regulations laid down by the Ministry of Agriculture with assistance from the local consortium). These laws are exceptionally stringent, even draconian, but for the consumer, at the end of the day, quality is in the hands of nature and the viticulturist, not the national laws laid down in Rome.

Even the innocent can work out that it would take a saint to completely rubbish part of their harvest in a good year. *Riserva* they may not aspire to, but no one is going to play down whatever cards they have been dealt with! Business is business, and we are thus not referring to those who every so often find a need to talk up what may simply be a perfectly acceptable table wine. It can be bottled as such, and sometimes benefit without the consortium's blessing.

Sfuso is, as much as anything in this modern age of recherché nostalgia, a cultural phenomenon. Given the desire for novelty, this can be made to appear somewhat trendy. But in reality it's far from being as modish as that. Some, seizing their chance, may suggest that *sfuso* is organic, though its creator might not claim as such, knowing that biological control, or a sustainable method of agriculture, represents pretty much what they practice while others merely preach.

Under threat from changing social patterns *sfuso* still hangs on, ignoring the hubris of the go ahead upstarts, retaining instead those remnants of an agricultural system that within living memory provided the backbone of the Italian economy. It has existed since time immemorial, and you will have to get your skates on to catch a glimpse of its passing, so rapidly is it disappearing.

Not that many are obsessed about such things, and you don't have to look very far to see why. Besides not needing a degree - and too many families misguidedly consider one of those the key to every successful future - you have to acquire a taste for the labour; the back breaking tillage that once gave you calluses, a permanent stoop, and a whole different way of life. Technology does mitigate many of these ancient burdens, but you still have to appreciate the fact that being the product, by and large of a once peasant community, it's nothing at all about those much abused words, *crus* and vintage; at least in the sense of age, and sophisticated waffle.

What we're about to consider is analogous to the French *vin ordinaire* - a cheap, generally young red wine, for ordinary use. But at once it is best to profess, and trust not falsely, that only the description is homologous when making a comparison to an Italian *sfuso*.

Subjective as this may be, the *vin ordinaire* most will have the misfortune to meet are an anaemic contrast to an honest *sfuso*. While it might be true that in the table wines of Languedoc or Provence one would expect to obtain a decent quaffing wine, those thin French wines that seem to clutter up the more northern provinces, would need a lot of work to bring them up to the standard of a robust Italian country wine.

Perhaps these points may appear a touch partisan, which is almost as enjoyable as being politically incorrect, but you may be disarmed by the point that conversely, with reference to 'Super Tuscans', there really seems no reason why anyone would pay the price of a Château Margaux for an average Pomerol!

After all, in Italy the exceptional Sassicaia, a wine blended from both cabernet varieties, is not classified as DOC or DOCG, and can only be referred to as *Vino da Tavola*. We'll leave you to ponder the paradox in that!

Putting these personal matters aside, there are some important aspects about *sfuso* that should be stated at once. It is not chasing medals or market output. Nor is it interested in product differentiation. You can't hang a tag on *sfuso*. It is what it is. Not even an ideal or a quality, only an entity. Specifically, its *raison d'être* is a speedy accompaniment to comestibles, the rather important matter of food.

While it cannot be completely divorced from wooden barrels, this in a sense is the one aspect that separates it from the commercial development of the product.

It is important to shortly elaborate on this a little in an effort to give *sfuso* a context in which we can explain the matter, as fine wines are particular, if not fastidious, about whom they share the table with.

III: Concrete and Wood

A potted history.

Let it be said straight away, that wood appears little in the production of *sfuso*. Amphion, it seems, no longer plays his lyre so sweetly that trees left the ground, and presented themselves to the carpenter - or perhaps, in this case, to the cooper!

Portland cement vats - it's difficult to call them barrels even when the early versions closely reflected the style - appears to be an unlikely substitute for wood, though in many cases its use has also been seriously reduced by the advent of stainless steel containers. In this modern age there's not much difference in the price between a costly hardwood and stainless steel, but as far as *sfuso* is concerned the latter is as long lived, and has in this age of environmental anxiety, other serious green advantages that will have to be addressed. In a true sense; however, neither has yet totally replaced the cement vat on the small *podere*, where it still functions adequately for the needs of the farmer, and where all the initial cost has long since been absorbed. Neither does a wine that is aged need to start life off in a wooden barrel, but more on that later.

As we won't be meeting much timber on this journey, if a great deal more of trees, and knowing that wood was once an essential aspect in the production of all wine, not just for the ageing properties extolled within, but also because for long periods no other satisfactory vessels existed. Consequently, we've reached a very moot point. A somewhat controversial one, where you might feel Benini leaning over your shoulder. The mention of wood and ageing will have drawn a long and disquieting look across his normally cheerful features.

There's no point in asking when man first developed the art of making a cask, or even how they came to arrive at the type of wood best suited for storing wine. One seriously doubts that anyone knows the answer. Oak is certainly durable, but a thousand year or so early example on which to postulate, won't turn up at Sotheby's. For that reason we'll give verification a miss, and rely on speculation.

However, this is not to overlook the tireless task of archaeologists who have determined some intermediate date for the first emergence of wine vessels, or made some tentative explanation of their evolution. They, it may be assumed, will readily admit the difficulty of the task, and the probability of yet undiscovered evidence.

Almost unbelievably, hollowed out tree trunks have been suggested for the transport of wine, but it is extremely unlikely that anyone considered it a satisfactory method for storage. Nor would wine skins, known to be of Syrian origin, have been more than a temporary means of transportation. As an essential part of a local economy the movement of any goods, especially liquids, must have represented an enduring problem. Conserving a precious vintage in later times was to prove even more difficult.

Those who adhere to Bacon's philosophy of empiricism: an inclination to believe that man can profit by practical experiments allied to rational analysis, and as theoretical modelling at that time had absolutely no advocates, it's possible to accept that if it worked you left well alone. So we can imagine that if in their early experiments someone suggested they use staves made from pine, like 'square wheels', such an idea had little chance of catching on.

And thereby hangs a tale.

Without doubt ceramic vessels have been in use for many thousands of years, and certainly for the holding and transport of wine, often over very great distances. Yet one of the earlier problems associated with the material appeared difficult to successfully resolve. To be of any value in the conveyance of wine the containers, of necessity, had to be air tight, and one of the ways they thought to bring this about was to line the vessel, and seal the cap, with pitch. As pitch is soluble in alcohol, and the wine became resinous, it could not have been appreciated by the customer, even if they were prepared to suffer the result. An odd reference of the period suggests the unlikely antidote of adding roasted salt (sic) to camouflage the taste. Surprisingly, such an evil solution seems to have persisted for some time, as there are also early references to strong imported wines entailing the necessity of dilution by seawater.

If anyone considers this a veiled dig at Retsina, a Greek white wine flavoured with pine resin, and usually surreptitiously retired to the darkest corner of the suburban sideboard to age for another generation, they're right. There have been too many throbbing heads to forgive them. Ex-teenagers, of a now uncertain age, will remember such dusty specimens often turning up at impromptu bottle parties, safely purloined in the knowledge that their parents would not question, or even regret, the mode of its passing.

Plausibly, and not surprisingly, the related sealing difficulty appears to have been one of those persistently retrogressive steps brought about by the unfortunate historical rise and fall of civilizations. In this way, satisfactory solutions to such intractable problems seem to have evolved merely to be subsequently lost.

In one such preceding millennium for example (c.3500 B.C.), finely worked jars in clay were being fired in what was to become Persia. Designed to lie on the side so the deposits could settle, they were sealed with a wet clay cap, kept damp and free of shrinking by retaining a horizontal position so the contents could maintain the stopper in a moist condition. Similar amphorae of a Greco-Egyptian form with the familiar pointed base, were certainly being used by the Etruscans in Tuscany, but whether they had successful seals is not so sure.

The Romans, on the other hand, were to become familiar with hooped barrels, a practice they may have learnt from the conservation of beer in northern Europe. We're on fairly safe ground in acknowledging that the Celts were excellent wood workers as well as brewers, implying that in four hundred B.C. the annual celebrity junket wasn't a thing to be missed. Therefore, a few odd centuries here or there in the development of the barrel will not make much difference to the narrative, even if it does to history.

However wooden barrels came about, the choice of deciduous oak and chestnut grown in temperate zones was fortuitous. Modern science has done its best to convince us of the attributes provided by such timber, but it's highly unlikely such esoteric matters influenced our pre-Christian forebears. It surely stretches the imagination to believe that some pagan flamen neglected the deity for long enough to discover a method of preserving their spiritual offerings. Nor that an ancient apothecary, searching for an 'elixir vitae', happily added his empirical results to the cauldron of knowledge.

That the Roman poet Horace's father was an apothecary in Venosa, a steep, bare town in Apulia, would be a romantic allusion to such authenticity, despite his young son developing a heady taste for elegant wines. Nor does the idea that wine barrels came about on the introduction of carvel built boats replacing those of clinker construction stand up to close scrutiny, as such a maritime change was not deemed to have taken place until the fourteenth century when wooden barrels had long been in service.

To abuse an epigram: The wine in the barrel will not quench our thirst! In which case we must press on.

Whatever its evolution, barrels became one of those essential requisites in viticulture. Man, without them, would have found it hard work developing wine into something of an art form. We can only thank some unrecorded genius with an excellent imagination for the concept. After all, the culmination of this technological artifice enabled the transition from the wine our Lord consumed to the fine wine gathering dust in vintner's dark, temperature controlled cellars.

That's a tidy journey, for as a traveller in Judaea's parched and tree-less places, despite the evolution transpiring in the north of Europe, Jesus would still have had the dubious pleasure of consuming wine stored in tar sealed ceramic vessels. There, in the provinces, it had also probably suffered the Roman practice of boiling the 'must', or grape juice before fermentation, down to one half, or even one-third, to give it longevity. It must have been an early miracle for Him to persuade timorous acolytes to develop a taste for such tipple, while it certainly seems to have convinced Mahomet to stick to coffee, and remain teetotal.

Despite the vagaries of this infamous Roman mode of protraction, we don't have to rely solely on legend to consider if it proved effective or not. Pliny the Elder, something of a trencherman compared to his more conservative nephew, has informed us that he had come across a wine made in the consulship of Opimius, 200 years previously. That he mentioned the fact, and drew no negative conclusions; suggest that the contents may have been, if not noteworthy, at least useful for blending with more recent wine. He sadly chose not to leave any tasting notes, and nor, as far as we know, do the makers of *sfuso*. They make wine to drink, and leave academic meditation to the imagination of others.

The reason for such a loquacious excursion into this

matter of timber, lies in the fact that though wooden barrels were long used for storing all wine, the transient quality of *sfuso* always argued for it being consumed within the year, and not truly dependent on wood.

Wine (and also beer in more northern climes) was presumably consumed where the quality of water was hardly considered reliable; therefore, the practical quantity of wine produced on small farms dictated the barrels they needed, besides being related to an amount they could afford. Wooden barrels can be prodigiously vast, but their cost is also prodigious in proportion - well beyond the pockets of a small farmer. That's an important distinction. In twelve months, the few barrels they possessed would, in all probability, be empty well in advance of any decline in the original quality of the wine.

So it's not surprising that impecunious small farmers, with no interest in ageing, or the expense of maintaining wooden casks, came in time to opt for the less expensive alternative of a substantial cement construction with an internal synthetic resin coating. If there is no desire to 'improve' the wine, or to reach some peak of perfection, then little is lost by 'reaching for the Portland'!

Podere vats

To his advantage, and with these affordable vats, the farmer can manage to produce a satisfactory quantity of wine for his daily needs. This is a crucial factor, for wine held in such containers continues to have a very limited life, and there is a historical tendency to consume the contents within the year, despite the possibility of a little more age. It is also a practical problem, for nature runs a tight schedule, and the next *vendemmia* in the twelve monthly cycle pre-supposes the vats will be empty. Despite this, such wine can be bottled, remaining palatable for a year or two more, but not many proprietors of a small farm would consider it worthwhile.

In any case, this is not the place to commence a discussion on the quality of one wine or another, wood or no wood. You would soon rumble the fact that 'this expert' is not qualified to undertake such a critique. Benini, in any case, would look askance at such presumption; seemingly stressing the belief that wine comes in only two types - *'buono'* or *'orrendo'*!

Tuscan farmers don't have time to waste on the particular.

Let's just say, one man's 'floral aroma with cherry notes' may, after all, be another man's poison. All we need consider is that no matter which wine we are discussing, such will be made from fermented grapes. Hence, with that in mind, 'all babies are born the same'. How they are nurtured will finally help us distinguish the one from the other.

IV: A Question of Identity.

So what exactly do I have in mind when trying to explain such a nebulous concept as *sfuso*?

To understand correctly we must return to the theme expounded in the first chapters: the distinction created by the decision to either consume the new wine after its second fermentation, or to save it for posterity.

In Italy, country folk have a tendency to refer to commercially produced wine intended for a future market as *lavorato*, or 'worked'. It may be kind to say that in this they are referring to the specialized craft necessary to take wine beyond the relatively straight-forward, if still arduous, creation of *sfuso*. Most have little interest in the barrique, small 225 litre casks of new oak where the wine can be aged for as little as six months to acquire taste, and avoid excessive oxidation. Nor indeed, for that matter, interest in any other period of wood ageing.

Despite this, displaying the shrewdness of their kind, they do recognize the qualities that make a great wine, even if they rarely have the opportunity of consuming one. The mention of Brunello di Montalcino will have Tuscans nodding their heads in respectful affirmation. That being so, it is a little sad to relate the criminal practice facetiously termed, 'Brunellogate' (2008), that saw one and a half million bottles of Montalcino wines declassified, with some being sent for distillation into commercial alcohol. No wonder the sceptical among us will continue to hold that the reputations of many are falsely held on the foundation of a name that is built on the pinnacle of a few.

Understandably, not so many are blessed with the wealth, or the inclination, to purchase their annual consumption in bottles obtained from casks of wood, but Italians will assure you that in this instance there is also the matter of a logical and valid interest in their health. It is not something to be dismissed lightly, especially when their point is honestly held. Still, it is difficult to believe that the French are the only hypochondriacs among us when the average Italian considers 37.5°C. definitely indicates the onset of a fever, and a notch higher requires the desirable presence of the *sacerdote*.

Whether this is fair or not, you should avoid drawing

the conclusion that Italians are parsimonious and 'precious'. The question of expense is not a factor in their apprehension, whereas metabolic reactions, and disturbances in the liver, most certainly are. Those little old ladies in black patiently working their way through the beads of their rosaries in the nation's churches may well be offering supplications for husbands who'd forgotten, in these wealthier modern times, the traditions and admonishments of their fathers.

Being traditionally sensible where alcohol is concerned, such a caveat merely translates into a strong belief that to absorb the quantity of wine used as the standard beverage in Italy, of a quality produced by the great wine estates (or even the lesser), is to risk a too early exit from the world. Best, they conclude, is to stick to the biblical offerings where the shortness of a life wasn't administered by cirrhosis of the liver, or a pocket as deep as the Monte dei Paschi di Siena bank.

Such convictions can be taken to extremes. Characteristically of any *festa*, and in the unlikely event that the wine on offer is a superb and expensive vintage, then regardless of any deference to quality the average Italian will hardly shrink from using water as a swift and effective chastener if they think it necessary. After all, who are we to criticize, when Anglo Saxons have been known to add Stone's Ginger Wine, let alone 'branch' water, to a single malt whisky!

There is; however, some international support for their point of view regarding the efficacy of wine, albeit with one caveat.

Research into groups that have a greater than average longevity of life seem to centre on those who have a Mediterranean diet: one high in fresh fruit and vegetables, olive oil, bread (no butter) and, of course, wine - very often two or three glasses per day. In Tuscany generally red, but in southern Italy as likely white. Whether they eat more meat or fish depends on where they live, but in either case it must not to be excessive.

The caveat?

The wine will rarely have come from a bottle with a label on it!

Their trick in drinking wine is to only have the glass one third full. In this way they can continue to replenish it through the meal, yet drink very little. This is the Italian way that avoids abandoning yourself to excess.

They are not particularly abstemious, but one learns very slowly the art of their life.

Whether you believe that wine is a catholicon or not is a personal matter of belief. At least in Italy they continue to say: *Buon vino fa buon sangue* - good wine makes good blood. But as we will see, the former does not necessarily refer to its cost.

For Italians of the countryside, and not a few in the cities as well, *comune sfuso*, the local wine, is what you drink as a family (*comune* used here: in the sense of something in common; available to everyone). Within this category, and its narrow time scale, there is one important nuance: those who like their wine sprightly and ebullient, and those of an opposite persuasion who like it muscular but tranquil. (The same some of us, naturally, are quite happy to have our feet in both camps!) This is conviction *sfuso* without a doubt, but we shouldn't press the point too hard.

Despite the fact that many a wiry, leathery farmer prefers his wine young and fresh, don't be misled into believing that it in any way resembles the precocious Beaujolais Nouveau, a modest French wine using the Gamay Noir grape. Being available as early as the middle of November, it is no more than an annual fashionable event in France, introduced into the United Kingdom by the late, droll and sagacious, Sir Clement Freud, to cheer the populace up before Christmas. Such wine is created using a particular method of vinification, and by the New Year is past its best, leaving the proper Beaujolais to be enjoyed at leisure.

Nor should *sfuso* be compared with any such wine that has an appellation. It is far more ubiquitous than that because, as you'll recall, it is not a region or a grape at all, merely the generic term for a myriad of varietal wines that are obtained 'loose' - very often from what resembles a petrol-pump!

In England, those of a half forgotten era, old enough to remember purchasing their tea and sugar loose from foil lined plywood boxes will readily understand the term *sfuso*. In Italy, for the same reason, when you talk about *sfuso* people assume in a psycho-suggestive way you are probably talking about wine. And wine is what's being metaphorically 'shovelled' into sundry miscellaneous containers.

One must confess, that to discuss *sfuso* critically

would seem hardly enlightening or worthwhile when the product has so little identity in marketing or promotional terms. What does one make of a noun that is an adjective or a verb - a name that can describe itself? How do you get to grips with such an elusive enigma where 'esoteric' perfectly describes a wine you can see and taste, but can't solicit, because it's like a mug without a handle?

Precisely. And where are you supposed to find the fountainhead - the source - of this authentic *sfuso*?

By now you may well have realized there's little point in searching through a telephone directory. Any reference to such an outlet will almost certainly be describing a middleman, and that is not likely to be a 'source' in terms of a producer. As 'local' is significant you might consider asking the local postman who surely must know everyone, but as they zoom around in a Fiat Panda, and the city sort will point you to an outlet, something more enterprising is needed.

There's the possibility that you may have already caught a glimpse of this definitive Tuscan character on a market day, parked on some windy street corner surrounded by others who might very well be the same.

Oh, you'll spot them all right. You can't really miss them. Raw characters, something like Fidel Castro without the beard, and just as sartorially dressed.

You will study them carefully and discreetly for two reasons. Firstly, one should avoid interrupting a conclave of farmers. How embarrassing could that be? Secondly, a dozen pedantic opinions may turn into an imbroglio from which no good will come!

Discreetly, you can naturally fall into conversation with one who appears friendly, but as he's of a sober nature, you need to approach him with all the finesse of a Hardy rod and line, whose bait is about to tickle a trout. Once hooked you will find him an affable and patient conversationalist. After all, he might need to translate what passes as fragments of impoverished Italian into a more comfortable dialect that would tax a professor of philology, let alone a solid man of the soil. But he'll try. Candid opinions are every Italian's raison d'être, and he'll welcome the chance to give them an airing.

This colloquial human 'grape vine' - a man of the *campagna* - a rural dweller used to a timeless way of life that breeds provincial self sufficiency and an estimable knowledge of country matters, describes a phrase that would have an Italian shaking their head in mystification. But that is what he is. Discreetly he will point you in the right direction, and if you're lucky, contrive an introduction. The jackpot would be if he turns out to be the proprietor of such a vineyard, and takes a shine to you. He then becomes, in the scale of things, somewhat higher than a successful premium bond.

Persuasion will never really be part of the message. Enthusiasm certainly, but no one is twisting your arm. *Sfuso* is a matter of fact business. After all, there is nothing competitive about sfuso. Local it may be, the true *vino da tavola* or table wine, and what you get, is what you drink.

Yet it is also true, that when the ingredients may be one, or the combination of two or three of the thousands of grape varieties in thousands of geographical variants, then some distinction must necessarily apply.

Of course, you can't try them all, so to avoid a possible nervous breakdown, or the rapid onset of family fatigue among members who have been envisaging sunny beaches not a collection of dusty *cantine*, just be satisfied to stay on your own substantial patch - or one or two removed - and try to remember which of those dusty white roads finally led you to Elysium.

For those less intrepid, and with little time in between cut-price flights, all is not lost, as every perceived opening has its entrepreneurs. Though they hardly jump out at you the chances are, that by keeping a beady eye open rather than a bleary one, you will come across those shops and co-operative outlets we've mentioned that sell *sfuso*. They are widespread, from chic to cheerful, and they are no bad place to start. The experienced haggler, disadvantaged perhaps by language, will still know that 'retailer' means overheads, with a greater need to turn a coin. But don't let that put you off. Such outlets will be nothing if not competitive. You may even have the benefit of a tasting on which to make your judgement, and very often a choice. Not something you can experience when taking a bottle down from a supermarket shelf.

These small outlets may vary from quaint shops hidden in medieval streets, to dusty warehouses on the edge of town. Some may even be purpose built near a strategic position, such as a carriage-way, to maximize trade. Not all will have a selection of local wines, but those that do will generally be willing to offer specific details of the grapes and the neighbouring vineyards that have supplied them.

Enoteca: Galluzzo, Florence.

Actual comparisons seem hardly pertinent. *Sfuso* is not wine to eulogize over, being a local wine for local people. It is certainly an acquired taste, but not one where you need to underline the nature of the matter. Like ducks we all, sooner or later, take to the water.

Benini will not have much to say about so strange a baptism!

And there's the rub. If you're reading this then it's likely you've never been the well-scrubbed Tuscan baby receiving spiritual purification (no pun intended) from Don Angelo, with as yet not a clue about those quaint liquid customs their parents indulge in; milk being your exclusive tipple. But in time they come to represent those delicate shades of Italian culture, including the local wine, that by some mysterious osmotic process is filtered gradually into the conscience, assimilated over those many years that we may have already lost. Such things will come naturally through childhood, youth and the chatter of enlightened elder siblings. Time and birthplace you may consider have not been on our side. We shall have to be swift if we're late learners.

Meanwhile, in both good years and bad years, the locals will talk about the historical fortunes of the weather, their triumphs and disasters, and be content to consume what the gods have ordained. They do it all without complaining, or taking their business elsewhere. There is no consortium or denomination for *sfuso*. No DOC or DOCG; coming only in the style of the man or woman who creates it. For them *sfuso* is part of their way of life, as is the story of Benini's wine.

Podere Sant'Anna, though its owners have long been dispersed through marriages or careers, remains a family farm - in the heredity sense that all the siblings retain a share - though as so often happens in contemporary times, none of the present generation have found it practical to make it their home. Individualism, the desire to fashion an independent way of life, has seen an understandable, but steady erosion of shared responsibility. Coming from the managerial classes they have taken to professional work that has left only room for the sentiment, and a waning doggedness to preserve the traditions of a vanishing way of life.

Benini, as the elder brother, has worked hard to sustain it, and though the body is in need of respite from the endless demands of his many interests, he will have been denied the chance of a short repose, for following behind the grapes will have come the other great pillar of the Italian rural economy, the harvesting of the olives. Neither is much mechanized on a small Tuscan podere, indicating four months of intense toil between September and Christmas. For this reason, in Italy, distant offspring are never too distant, often called from some far-flung corner of the nation to roll up their sleeves, and set to work. Despite the luxury of technical innovation and sedentary occupations, the harvest with timeless precedence has not yet quite lost its place in the nation's affections.

Meanwhile, in Tuscany, the once vibrant colours of the land have given way to the quiet decline of old age; stealthily the shadows were lengthening between the silent rows of vines as the earth leant back on its axis, reaching out for its greatest declination. A silence you could almost inhale had descended over the small *podere* sheltering under the steep slopes that rose sharply behind. A silence that is broken only by the wind; a sound that is not musical like the warm *scirocco* coming out of northern Africa, but the deep moaning breath of the *grecale* that surges through the densely shrouded branches of the cypress trees, buffets the guttering of the eaves, and echoes in the empty barns from where the grain has long departed. Leaves, like agitated small birds, swirl round in the tiny piazza, lifting off only to settle down again in a momentary stillness. There is something both mysterious and profound in this tired resignation of nature. It seems that there has hardly been time for reflection on what has past, for in early December Benini had driven down the tall avenue of cypress trees, past the little family chapel with its derelict *bocciodromo*, or bowling alley, to stand behind the blackened parade of twisted trunks that seem to totter down the hill. He is here in the vineyard, with his acolyte, to make a decision.

Mysterious? Certainly, and through the coming seasons it was slowly revealed what a long and arcane process the making of wine really is. Nor can one imagine the essential continuity; the long sequel of events that ensures for the men and women who tend the vines, that today is really only the beginning of tomorrow. A good enough reason one would half expect, for the wind and silence to accompany a welcome, if ephemeral pause, in their external industry.

It might have - except that in the *cantina*, or cellar, a patient and constant vigilance was taking place over their far from sleeping creation. Having given it life, they must now tend to its survival.

It also explains why Benini came to be there, still a solitary figure, ruminating it seemed on the intentions of the land. Perhaps his thoughts were merely reflections on the triumphs and tribulations of the fast diminishing year. Not something he could easily share, being more esoteric than practical. Yet, at the same time, it appeared as though he was contemplating nothing more onerous than having his car MOT'd, hoping for good news, knowing it would probably present a few surprises.

But a rural economy isn't quite like that. You can't simply slap a new tyre on nature. Months of hard work can be left devastated by unexpected violent storms, or remain fruitless by a protracted summer without the essential spring rain.

Tuscans still mutter grimly about the terrible frosts that came in January 1985 destroying vast tracts of olive groves, and thus the harvests for five years - that being the time it takes for an olive tree to reach maturity.

Though a contemporary disaster, it pales into insignificance when compared to the northern European winters of the Middle Ages. They were so severe in the fifteenth and sixteenth century, that in Flanders the wine had to be cut with hatchets, and starvation was rife as whole harvests failed.

These are the shared traumata of every farmer. As in classical times they can never be sure what Demeter, the Goddess of agriculture, will have in store for them.

All you are likely to gather from Benini is that this capricious divinity's daughter, Persephone, the goddess of spring, will hopefully not neglect to visit Sant'Anna if they're to expect an excellent harvest

There are still those who, perhaps tongue in cheek, insist that a crop of red poppies scattered across the mustard coloured cornfields in June, signal her omniscient benefice. Well, this is Italy, and though the Greek goddess is a renascent Roman goddess, Ceres, perpetuated in the word cereal, this is still reason to hope she will continue secretly to cast her ancient spell over the efforts of the present agricultural community.

But on a dreary and overcast winter's day, you're rather more inclined to believe that the dull spectrum visible before your eyes, suggests Benini would have to rely on the efficacy of his own good judgment - or the toss of a coin.

Much of his highly vocal rumination will be influenced by the environment, even if now merely a subconscious contribution to the process. Nature, Benini warns, always insists on retaining the arbitrary privilege of the last word. When you'd like sun, you can be sure of rain! Viticulture, so they say, is like tickling a cat's stomach. Loving the attention, you never know when it will suddenly tire and scratch you.

There seems only one thing the farmer can, more or less, depend on. Not one hundred percent - but with experience, near enough. Returning to the *cantina*, Benini explained that to master the making of wine it's essential to understand the nature of the soil in which the grapes will grow.

Like any plant, you might think, from roses to rhubarb.

He's not likely to welcome the knowing smile on your face. Being mildly pedantic, he will obstinately insist in being prepared to go to some considerable length to make sure you are fully apprised of the geographical and historical subject matter that determines and supports his husbandry.

No sliding off now.

Benini will carefully point out that Sant'Anna is

situated on the gently sloping agricultural land of a very old *podere*, or small tenant farm, often one of several belonging to a larger estate known in Italy as an *azienda agricola* - the legendary, and sometimes infamous, *fattoria*.

To understand these rudiments of history you need to appreciate the character of these modest farms. As such, they recall the country's feudal rather than yeoman past, a past that hardly reflects propitiously on the very ancient nature of the nation.

The Lombards in the sixth century, having seized sizeable pieces of land from the indigenous population, settled in the area, creating estates between the Alps and the Po River. Instead of claiming the historical one-third portion of land for themselves, they changed this to one - third of the produce of the land. The original owners were; therefore, forced to share the benefits of their labour. In many cases the nature of the terrain favoured very large estates much in the manner of the original Roman system called *Latifundium*, where cereal and grass rotation predominated. However, the indolence of these feudal lords didn't last long, but the method appealed to robber barons south of the Apennines, who were busy carving out substantial domains for themselves. They were infinitely more successful than these northern interlopers, and so it remained from the eighth century until the tenants were finally released from their vassalage after the Second World War when agricultural reforms - *riforma agraria* - created an abundance of small independent farms, such as the one the Benini family own.

And they are small, very often only fifty hectares - one hundred and twenty-five acres. In the modern Italy, one would be hard pressed to make a living on something so restricted. It's a fact born out by the abandoned farm houses sitting sadly and unwanted on isolated knolls with their shutter-less, empty windows; roofs seemingly collapsed from the weight of the sky; bare stones that once met somewhere - now nowhere. Void of life, and of lives, their occupants have been scattered to the new world, and the land given over to a more successful demesne.

Still just within living memory, the *mezzadria* contract between the landlord and farm worker (*contadino*) was made with the head of the family; all the family thus being bound by the contract which may have meant as much as an exacting 50% (*mezza*, as in half) of the produce of their labour going to the landlord. In the United States 'sharecropping' fulfilled a similar role, and came to an end roughly about the same time. Large families were thus at a premium as they could obtain a larger farm, or expand a smaller one. Such expansion can be seen in random multiple extensions that have created eccentric architectural forms in many Tuscan country buildings.

Abandoned farmhouse: ad hoc annexes.

It seems from this, that historically, the benefits of diverse crops and large unit productivity have been commonly recognized, as Sant'Anna itself, has a farm-house comprising 700 square metres on two floors - some 7535 square feet, representing a very large building. Even for a local nabob!

It's not known if this spacious, isolated building, protected by a bank of cypress trees to the northeast, and lying open to the sun on the south, was built to accommodate the marital alliances of one family or, unusual in Tuscany, constructed as purpose built multiple family units. On the plains of the Po River it was common, huge villa sized houses that were mere dormitories built round a courtyard. In Tuscany a sense of individualism seems to have survived the heavy hand of serfdom. You might work indirectly for one of the great land owners: a Medici, a Piccolomini or a Guidi; or perhaps one of the expanding city bourgeoisie who were buying up small portions of old estates, but you worked in your own way on a small plot of land that was your own responsibility, and paid your rent in kind.

In a completely new age, Benini's father acquired the property as his family home. Such had been the inevitable effect of technology and mechanized power replacing both man and beasts, that only one farm worker was required. The fact that it has a small chapel would suggest that at some time the farm probably housed enough people to be served by a peripatetic curate sent out from the local church. With such a captive audience, he'd have arrived very swiftly by bicycle down the hill, and more slowly, pushed the offertory of eggs and vegetables all the way back. In former days he may even have had recourse to a horse as they were an agreeable mode of transport, even if considerably more trouble than some air in the tyres, and a drop of oil on the chain. These accommodating steeds were still in use as carriers in Tuscan country places until the mid twentieth century.

The inclination of the hillside faces south and a little east; usefully being able to take advantage of all the available sun traversing across the face of the farm in a great swathe of penetrating light. This is not soft rolling countryside in the English sense, or even that of Middle Tennessee. Here the roll tends to disappear precipitously towards the invisible valley floor, seemingly curling dangerously under itself - a strong, bare countryside, with restless hills breaking like waves against the skyline.

Benini gestures expansively at the rapidly steepening land behind, to the small village near its top. It is almost hidden by the surrounding forest and countryside, a dark cluster of buildings with the sooty Torre Saracini, an old medieval tower constructed by a Tuscan grandee who seems to have spent most of his time in constant altercation with Florence and Pisa, to absolutely no avail, being soon dispossessed.

The village lies at 400 metres, about 100 metres above and behind Sant'Anna. Here it receives the warm, but turbulent south westerly *libeccio* coming off the Mediterranean Sea; the occasional *maestrale*, a cold, blustery north westerly wind; the dreaded north easterly *grecale*, and the warm westerly *ponente*, which crosses the Ligurian coast and wraps itself around the southern Apennines. Most importantly, some protection is offered from the fearsomely cold *tramontana* blasting over the Alpine peaks, the temperature plummeting ever lower, depressed by the wind's violent and extraordinary velocity. Any laundry surviving on the line, glaciated into rigid forms by this Siberian embrace, will ring like a bell in its belfry.

Despite such a breezy position, Benini maintains the farm is an attractively situated, but typically heterogeneous upland Tuscan site. And so it proved to be. The winter might have been chilly, but supported by a mild spring and a tolerable autumn, the summer in between was long and hot.

This was not entirely down to luck. A sunny orientation was ardently sought all over Europe where vines were to be cultivated; demonstrated even in far away England by the 2-4th century Roman vineyards of Bath, planted on the south-facing lower slopes of Lansdown. The area opposite the Paragon is still known locally as 'The Vineyards', but nowadays if you found a grape there, it probably came from Sainsbury's. Nevertheless, at least as late as the eighteenth century it was noted for the production of black cluster and muscadine grapes yielding 69 hogsheads (17,000 litres) and shipped out of Bristol at 10 guineas a hogshead. A bottle of wine, at perhaps a shilling, was nothing to get excited about when farm labourers were on ten pence a day, with beer money in the winter.

Such anecdotes are not things that trouble Benini much. All he ponders, is that having availed himself of a warm site, his father must have also considered what lay beneath his feet.

Well, there are quite a lot of important aspects to be noted about soil, besides being messy, muddy and very useful for testing Land Rovers! One shouldn't say that to Benini, of course. He's well into his didactic stride by now.

In keeping with the prevalent type of soil in this area, Sant'Anna is a potter's paradise of viscous clay. It would be, that is, except for the rare addition of deposits referred to as *Ghiaioso Rosso,* or red gravel, capable of doing terrible things to any pug mill.

The local copper mines, an industry from Etruscan times, are situated on the higher ground above the town. Copper was worked in pre-Dynastic Egypt as an essential ingredient in the making of bronze, and no doubt this was also the Etruscan reason for mining the ore. Their important city of Populonia on the coast, close to the island of Elba, was famous for its metal industry; a processing facility where the local mine could probably deliver its ores for smelting. Now worked out or closed, the waste from their industry has been gradually dispersed over a large area by the elements and the natural movement of the earth's surface. This is hardly 'environmentalist friendly' being an unseen benefit from an early example of the poet William Blake's evil, 'satanic industries', for when gravel finds its way into clay, the heavy material remains conveniently open, providing efficient drainage in an otherwise impermeable earth.

Such a worthy characteristic was much appreciated by farmers. Human nature, being what it is, led to many seeking to replicate what couldn't have naturally occurred in the soil. The most important aspect of this enterprise depended for its success on being completely without charge!

Before tar macadam eliminated road gravel in Britain, highway maintenance workers were prone to leave such beneficial material scattered about. Others with an equal need, flirting with the risk of being transported to the colonies, sensibly appropriated this superfluous material for the benefit of a rural economy.

Whether, on the ubiquitous 'white roads' of Tuscany, dusty and milled by three thousand years of itinerant activity, similar measures provided agrarian peasants with the means to create sufficient marl for their needs, seems not to be recorded.

The gravel at Sant'Anna is immediately noticeable because of its appearance and colour; as you can imagine, a strong rusty red. In addition, there are other important minerals besides the copper hiding away out of sight, particularly iron.

These naturally occurring elements don't seem to have

unduly affected the water. Indeed, such are the local misgivings about 'mains water', and its occasional murky content, that there is a renaissance in natural mineral water. Free drinking water fountains, generously and suspiciously supplied by the local Water Board have recently appeared.

The only disappointment is the dispenser manages to look like a species of metal dustbin, instead of being a traditional edifice in solid local stone, durable, and capable of lasting in the Etruscan manner. Within a short time its rusting carcass will probably look too unhealthy to use!

Benini is quite happy to have his supply filter down the hillside, eventually arriving at Sant'Anna where it makes a useful contribution to the vineyards irrigation.

No one has managed to explain why, perversely, the *podere* well in its little piazza always seemed to be as dry as a bone, while the soil in the vineyard squelched under foot!

Though clay is cold and sticky in spring, and far from ideal when planting - somewhat like dibbling in glue - it has the contrary advantage of retaining moisture in the summer. This makes clay somewhat more serviceable than the other prevalent soil variety of this area.

During the tertiary period, sixty five million years ago, the region was deep under the sea. At some time tectonic plate movements pushed what is now Italy out of the water - the squeezed centre being the Apennine chain of mountains - leaving behind marine fossil shells to decorate just about all the old stone buildings and paved *piazze* in the area. However, as an alternative, there is an awkwardly deep stratum of sand. Sand, being mainly silica - see them as minuscule, amorphous glass beads - doesn't retain water. Possibly useful as an abrasive, but is a distinct disadvantage if you're contemplating a vineyard.

For this reason, despite its heavy nature, the local farmers prefer to work with clay, providing a soil type rich in plant food.

Benini, muttering in exasperation at all this intractability, is following in a long tradition, and has much to say on the matter. For millennia others, like him, have struggled and schemed to gain the upper hand.

For his part, Benini happens to be much enamoured

of beans!

Well, yes. So are many others, imagining the delicious *Fagioli in Fiasco - cannellini*, or white beans, cooked in a glass bottle and easily recognized if you're a habitué of Italian *trattorie*.

Benini is not amused. He has something else in mind, and it has little to do with what he perceives as facetious English humour.

Firstly, he insists, they improve the physical quality of the soil, and secondly, they increase its fertility. As he doesn't use the same legume for both, we'll sadly have to get stuck into the lupins.

His Roman forbears liked their soil free for vines - that is, easily crumbled when dry, glutinous when wet. To attain this improvement, one of the methods they utilized was the planting of lupins. When the crop was mature it could be ploughed into the soil as a green fertilizer.

How they stumbled upon this is not known, being unlikely they knew anything so esoteric as the fact that lupins managed to nourish the soil by fixing the nitrogen from the atmosphere into ammonia. The Enlightenment, and a passion for science, was still a very long way off.

There are well over two hundred species of lupins, the local variety being known as *Sulla*. The tops are used for animal fodder, the roots as a green manure.

Neither did Benini look kindly on suggestions that the one obvious quality of lupin seeds is that they're as hard as bullets, and quite equal to passing themselves off as gravel, if not for anything else! Whether they would manage to keep the soil open in such a manner, remains uncertain!

Meanwhile, it probably helps to explain the magenta coloured blanket of flowers bursting over the road-side banks of Tuscan byways; result of an agricultural practice that seems to have continued despite the advent of modern methods, as one still sees whole fields given over to these beans.

Despite their dubious compatibility, lupins and wine have an ancient recorded history. The Greek Stoic philosopher, Zeno, was said to have described himself as resembling lupin seeds, because when he had been well soaked in wine, he felt less bitter. As he was famous for reducing every argument to nothing, the story may appear apocryphal, as lupins never seem to have been much used in the human diet, soaked in wine or otherwise. Though you never can tell with stoics.

As his near contemporary, Plato, held wild opinions on Atlantis, philosophers are best not trusted in these matters. Which doesn't say a great deal for cooked lupin seeds that have lately become commercially available in the belief that they aid the absorption of cholesterol. The transmuted attributes of red wine would appear more beneficial - having the added advantage of not giving you indigestion!

Before the chemical revolution, which led to synthetic fertilizers, they found they could turn clay into good soil by burning the wood collected from the pruning of vines or olive trees, and turning the burnt embers into the soil. Like so many other agricultural practices, this probably originated with the Romans, especially in their northern colonies where the planting of vines called for special attention to the soil. Admittedly, this simple process is a long way from the complicated procedures Edwardian gardeners were said to have concocted, where clay was sprinkled with fine coal dust and added to the pyre, before being covered with layers of leaf mould and turf. Their efforts seem to have more in common with the Italian *carbonari*, the charcoal makers, a practice, if not already dead, at least a dying process. Nor, come to think of it, could they ever have contemplated using this method to improve the ten-acre field down at 'Folly Bottom'!

The tradition of burning still marginally continues in Tuscany. Little bonfires are occasionally still to be seen, lit at the point where a new vine is to be planted.

You might believe such things were long past.

Well, a great deal of this immemorial rural ingenuity, may still be harboured in the soul of the farmer, for Benini was discovered on one cold morning sheepishly tending a small blaze among the vines as though he was making an offering to some ancient and benign god, as most surely and sympathetically he could have been. He hastily explained that it was no such thing, given that the benefits of this practice had been recognized for thousands of years in the purifying fires of the Greek heroes. The principle being that the carbon absorbed all sorts of impurities, and sweetened the soil.

That being the case, it can certainly be no bad thing in such terrain.

VI: Genesis. Birth of a Vineyard

Benini's presence at Sant'Anna hadn't been to take part in some primaeval rite, though no doubt observances in times past perplexed farmers as much as they do now. It seems reasonable to suppose that supplicants must always have pondered earnestly on what must be the necessary moment to coax the annual cultivation of vines into life. Once upon a time this took a lot of hand wringing, oblations and prayers. Today, we only think we know better.

He was treading on hallowed ground. Planted and organized by his father some fifty years previously when the farm was of a much larger acreage, it had obviously come to represent a great deal of Benini's own personal history.

As in all such ventures there had been the arduous proving of standard agricultural practices that either worked on this plot, or they didn't. Most of these elements, for the novice, require a great deal of attention if they are to make something of them. As the information is being orally described, it's quite possible that even a northern Italian, faced with the preponderance of colloquial expressions, might not entirely understand, and would thus necessitate a circuitous debate on their precise meaning. Conversations were thus very long, and occasionally exasperating.

Nevertheless, Benini's, explanation on the work involved revealed an interesting insight into the unexpectedly methodical character of Tuscan *podere* cultivation; a discipline that turns out to be completely in tune with the elements of the seasons. That is just as well, as Mother Nature seems to determine every facet of its existence.

It must be said that what follows is a little academic, as the planting of new vineyards has been halted by a present European Community edict. The only concession is that when a vineyard is taken out of cultivation its acreage can be transferred elsewhere on the farm, or even sold to another vineyard. There is a moratorium of five years before this decision becomes absolute. As one might expect in this twilight of the *podere*, mostly the vineyard, or a specific acreage of vines, get sold.

So, if you fancy a few choice rows of Sangiovese in your garden, it's recommended you have a quick look at the E.U. CAP reforms on terrain morphology and vine cultivation. If it doesn't provide a little comfortable bedside reading, then beware the stuff of nightmares!

This effort in controlling the market, and halting the supposed burgeoning sprawl, takes little consideration of the fundamental reality that if a product is not cost effective then inefficient producers will eventually fall by the wayside, allowing the market to find a sustainable level. The modern intrusion of supermarket influence on prices places a large enough burden on the producer without the suffocation of artless government interference. A taxation regime seems quite sufficient.

Agriculture is not a constant like automobiles or television sets where, to some degree at least, the manipulation of production levels can be applied to accommodate the demands of less than discriminating consumers. Those who are familiar with a so called 'equilibrium market price' in which the quantity demanded is exactly the quantity supplied, know that in the real world of turnips, potatoes - and in this case, grapes - such economic terms are irrelevant. You can encourage nature, but it's impossible to make it conform exactly to your wishes. A glut today is as likely a famine tomorrow.

These small Tuscan farms, with no ambition to increase production, are not actually affected by such economic mayhem. But at least to the bureaucrat's satisfaction, they won't be tempted to sneak in another row of vines.

In any case, eventually such laws will probably come to nought, being similar to those laid down by that most pitiless of emperors, Domitian. Fearful that agriculture in general was being neglected, and vineyards too much cultivated, he prohibited their planting in Italy, and more disastrously, that half be cut down in the provinces. Needless to say, as soon as the emperor was no more, neither were his laws.

One always has the feeling that legislation is enacted for the benefit of some to the disadvantage of others, and control always seems to have loomed large in the making of wine. Adam Smith, probably the most influential political economist since Aristotle, advancing his theory on a market economy, describes how the vineyard was considered the most valuable part of the farm. In 'The Wealth of Nations' published in 1776, he states: 'In France the old landed proprietors of vineyards were moved to prevent the planting of new ones, obtaining an order of council 'prohibiting both the planting of new vineyards, and the renewal of those old ones, of which the cultivation had been interrupted for two years without a particular permission from the king, to be granted only in consequence of an information from the 'intendant' of the province, certifying that he had examined the land, and that it was incapable of any other culture'.

Smith goes on to note that the 'pretence' of this order was given as the scarcity of corn and pasture due to the super abundance of wine. Needless to say, he went on to abrogate the basis of the argument.

If the bureaucrats in Brussels indulged in a little timely research, it would reveal to them that on his demise even the memory of Domitian was rigorously expunged from the record. History, those sages should note, has a habit of repeating itself.

Such totalitarian edicts that might beset the planting of the Benini vineyard, at the time did not exist. Shortly after the Second World War, governments had too much on their plates to concern themselves with the minutia of agricultural activity, only the wider aspect of supply, and the European Market had not yet blossomed into its Orwellian manifestation of a Union. Just returning the land to some sort of productivity was sufficient; which is precisely where we'd left Sant'Anna, and Benini's commentary on planting a new vineyard.

Remembering that the farm has the important aspect of laying open to the sun, adversely, the neighbouring irregular precipices of land, sometimes like rollers on a stormy sea, rearing and looping into dark shadowy troughs, are only fertile enough to provide lush grazing for the use of once immigrant Sardinian shepherds who tend their sheep on the downs, enabling them to produce from the ewe's milk a variety of popular Pecorino cheeses. Even when naturally terraced, the viticulturist will give such places a wide berth if the topography entails casting a gloomy shade over the vines. The sun is everything - on both sides of the aisle!

When the terrain is compacted it serves no useful purpose for the cultivation of plants. Falling out of a fig tree here can do terrible things to your skeletal system. That established, something must be done to make it acceptable for the growing of vines.

While the preparation of the vineyard, or *vigneto*, is particular to every *podere*, all their ancestors seem to have learnt from behind the same Tuscan plough. In this it generally follows the basic agricultural practice for the area.

Given the previous remarks on the composition of the soil, this particular landscape doesn't present the farmer with a primrose path. But some are fortunate. The orientation places part of Sant'Anna on a piece of relatively level ground, dropping away gradually on three sides to its perimeter giving, in effect, a wide promontory on which the farmhouse also sits.

Benini makes the work sound relatively simple, but after a lengthy discourse on the matter, in retrospection it may be considered that he understates the sheer physical effort of the accomplishment.

What follows is the initial laying out of a vineyard; groundwork that will contain elements of the essential preparation needed every successive year.

The soil in the selected ground has first to be bulldozed into a uniform surface, as the days of planting vines simply in the nearest ditch, have long past. Whereas in medieval times you might have scratched a decent hole in the ground, inserted the cutting, and relied on nature to do the rest, now the soil preparation alone takes considerable time.

For this uniformity the wide, squat caterpillar tractor that make the white roads of Tuscany a teeth-rattling experience, come into their own. That they almost defy gravity says much for their utilitarian popularity, and as they were often the only mechanized vehicles available, became the veritable 'maid of all work'. Once, you might even have seen *'la signora'* perched on the back for a trip to the bus stop. Now these stalwart feminine souls dart around in a Fiat Panda, as though it were a bulldozer!

Being the only vehicle capable of working what appear to be near vertical inclines defining much of the surrounding terrain, bulldozers will thus make short work of any field that has a mere hint of being level. Tractors with tyres have all the mod con's: air conditioning, dust filters, infinitely variable transmission and quadrophonic whatever, but nothing seems to shake the farmer's affection for these cranking, grinding, Herculean monsters, even if they loosen his dental machinery.

Fiat bulldozer.

Having created this uniformity by first lightly turning over the soil, towards the end of August the farmer, perversely, sets about roughing the soil up again. Turned over into one metre deep furrows, it's a mountainous sight that puzzles those who lack the experience of working such heavy land. Clay is a most cantankerous material with a stubborn tendency to resist being penetrated by water. Yet, when it has, being reluctant to let it out again.

After one of those long hot summers the topsoil will have been baked hard to some depth, and seemingly, having by-passed that pug, mostly resembles a brick! The only way to purify the soil, and let the air in, is to open it by an aggressive *scasso del terreno,* which is best described as 'scouring the earth'.

To attain a workable soil, the area continues to be regularly ploughed, interspersed with a further refining by the use of a harrow, so that by February or March of the following year, it is beginning to represent a smooth, friable, and uniform surface.

When they say 'timeless' in respect of the Tuscan countryside, they're probably intimating that farming in this area tends to be a protracted business. Accepting that something like this description must also have been true for the farming of grain before they systematized the land for vines, the coupling, and even tripling, of oxen yoked to the plough must have been a weary and onerous task. Sixty years ago, and even less, they could regularly be seen in Tuscany hauling ploughs and hay wagons, and to this day make an entrance during the *Palio* in Siena pulling the *carroccio*, originally a mobile altar carrying the battle standards of the *comune*.

One end of the proposed vineyard is then squared at 90 degrees, and the distance between the rows established giving due attention to the size of machinery used to tend the vineyard, which in its mature state has approximately 2.5 metres between the forty-four rows of vines of about 50 metres in length. If that doesn't seem too much, take into account that it represents 0.5 hectares (1.25 acres) and two thousand vines under cultivation. The rows are perfectly straight, being formed by the classical and simple surveyor's method of sightings using striped ranging poles. Having taken Imperial Roman roads in pretty much of a straight line across Europe, and all over the then known world, it is more than adequate for this purpose.

Straight is perhaps a little pedantic. The Romans weren't so insensitive that they couldn't deviate if necessary; cranking their way round the odd hill like Silbury, a puzzling neolithic site in north Wiltshire that possibly indicated their deference to the religious significance of the mound. Imperial engineers didn't have time to admire the terrain, or consider if vines grew happily on chalk. Grapes were doing quite well in '*Aquae Sulis*' down the road where the foot weary surveyors had the advantage of being able to have a hot bath when they needed one. (Those following in the footsteps of the Roman surveyors will be glad to know that Bath still has hot baths, but sadly no commercial vines.)

The specifications for the vineyard are of some moment, and historically we have an excellent idea of those used two thousand years ago by the Romans in the rich terrain of Campania.

If you are fortunate enough to visit the excavations of Pompei, at some point you will be heading in the direction of the amphitheatre. Just behind is a closed off area designated the Foro Boario, which despite its name indicating a cattle market, appears to enclose a neat modern vineyard. The vines; however, have been newly planted to a measurement determined by the archaeologists who excavated the site - that is 1.2 metres between the vines (approximately 4 *pes*, or 4 Roman feet) and 1.5 metres between the rows (approximately 1 *passus*, or one step of a Roman soldier.) As the latter is very narrow we can assume that its husbandry was exclusively down to manual, generally slave labour - unless they used a smaller animal, such as a mule, to pull a plough, as there was surely not enough room for an ox. Close by, the Porta Sarno is also an area given over to the study of ancient viticulture.

Primi pali.

This is the classical system for laying out the vineyard, and at Sant'Anna each row commences with a three metre high heavy stake, known appropriately as the *primo palo,* dug in for one metre at an angle of ten degrees back from the vertical. (At the opposite end, the *ultimo palo* is the same) These are anchored deep in the earth by a wire stay tethered to a large rock, of which rather too many are annually unearthed by the plough.

Lighter vertical poles are spaced at approximately five metre intervals, with thick robust bamboo canes interspersed at varying heights to supply added support for the vine. As small plantations of cane are commonly found along roadside ditches, having a tendency to grow naturally in damp areas, the farmers may have encouraged them for this, and other agricultural purposes.

In Italy, the words *primo* and *ultimo* have often figured in diverse, and attractive ways. When large families were the norm, they often resorted to, what would seem to us at least, the peculiar habit of naming their children by consecutive numbers.

Octavian had the title Augustus thrust upon him, though he was still Octavian to his chums. To Anglo-Saxon ears they have a pleasantly melodic sound: Primo, or Primella if a girl, Secondino or Secondina, and so on. They don't seem to have gone much above ten, as Decimo, hopefully for the mother, was Ultimo, or the last son. There may be other variants. In Tuscany, Finimola can also indicate the last female offspring. (A more complete list can be found in the appendix.)

How they ascertained who was going to be the last sibling has not been disclosed. It's not the only anomaly. After all, if you happened to be born at Easter in Italy, there was always the chance of being named Pasquale, after *Pasqua*, the Italian for Easter.

Returning to the matter of vines. The sides of the holes for the heavy upright stakes, standing between the angled first and last *pali*, are maintained as upright as possible in an effort to create a firmness that prevents shake. Anyone who has attempted to dig a deep hole will confirm that it tends to get wider, very much wider, at the top. For this purpose conical holes will not do, being inherently weak. But all is not lost. In the empirical world of the past, problems may have taken a little longer to solve, but they were, very often, in a distinctive way.

To facilitate this awkward work with the least disturbance to the surrounding soil, farmers pressing their minds to the task devised a special implement called a *cartoccio*. Its name comes from the shape of the blade that vaguely resembles a scroll (cartouche) curling towards the centre, and holding the soil firmly within its embrace from a vertical thrust, rather than with a tipping lift executed by a flat blade. This can still be hard work; its technical efficiency thwarted by hidden stones, or if the weather has been particularly wet, then the spades embrace will be a little too affectionate, being reluctant to release the damp earth.

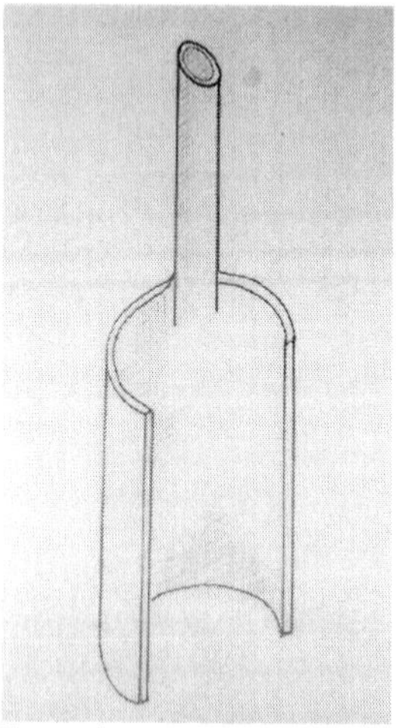

Cartoccio.

For the awkward interruption of stones and rocks they've devised another tool that might well have found service in a Hollywood 'shield and sandal' movie. The *vangheggia* is a long forged iron bar with an integrally wrought, strongly shaped arrowhead at the end. In effect, it is a spear. With forceful thrusts, the implement can be worked alongside, loosening the impediment to break up the blockage. It can be imagined that in the unsettled times Tuscany has encountered throughout its history, such an implement came easily to hand, serving the dual purposes of husbandry, and defence, admirably.

The *'primi'* and *'ultimi' pali* have three holes, approximately 30 cm apart, bored in the timber close to the top in a vertical line. Through these will be laced the wires along which the vines will grow, tensioned by rotating a simple 'L' shaped handle. The zinc-plated wires are fixed to the inner poles with staples, called *cambretta* (Colloquially, in Tuscany it is sometimes referred to as *gambretta*, which rather painfully describes the pinching powers of larger crustaceans. Not the diminutive shrimp or prawn - *gamberetto* - but the bad tempered *gambero*, or crayfish, to which it could originally have alluded.)

However, they are not tightly pinched, allowing a modicum of movement along the length when slack is taken up. That's about as high-tech as you can get with a *'primi'* or *'ultimi' pali.*

There are still plenty of wooden poles, treated with preservatives, in general use. They have an advantage in proving comfortable to handle, are easy to repair, and come in sizes to suit. After ten years or so, their strength suspect, and leached of all their protection, they will still find a use - finally being cut up to provide logs for a winter's fire.

Though concrete stakes reinforced with iron rods were introduced after the Second World War, the cement soon crumbled, allowing the exposed rods to oxidize and quickly deteriorate. After a day's work embedding them, the skin of the hands must have been severely flayed, which could hardly have endeared them to anyone. Examples still remain, often held up merely by the wires they were meant to support.

Modern, perfectly manicured vineyards, with short zinc plated steel poles running in perfect symmetry over the hillsides, indicate modern mechanized methods where both control and growth are optimized. Such systems are not often found in a small vineyard where the family might constitute the only labour available. Here the vines are often trained to two metres in height, providing a sufficient quantity of grapes from a restricted acreage, but proving more labour intensive in their preparation for the harvest.

Similarly at Sant'Anna, despite the assistance of machinery lifting the burden of the initial labour, in time honoured fashion, the vineyard had been carefully laid out like its ancestors, and finally made ready for the essential purpose of planting.

To this quite different enterprise, we must now turn our attention.

VII: A mixed case of Agronomics

Central Italy is not always warm, and the planting of young rooted cuttings, called *barbatelle* generally takes place after the possibility of frosts. Such work in the zone of Sant'Anna is very often accomplished in early spring, around March. The holes for these cuttings are between 50 - 60 cm. deep, and a little over 100 cm. (c.3.3 feet) apart. One wonders if the latter represented the standard pace of the farmer, or that a convenient stick came to hand on the day, as such finicky, scrupulous precision wouldn't have concerned a *podere* worker that much when exact measurement was something quite different from the accepted rule.

Well, times have changed. For the modern work of planting, where something more substantial than a garden dibber is needed, a mechanical drill conveniently and automatically makes the holes.

Having previously been churlish about sand, Benini now has to admit that it does have some uses. An example is that before the cutting is inserted fine sand is poured into the cavity to allow the young roots to muscle their way about more easily during the first few months of propagation.

Later; however, when the vineyard is established, if a new rooted cutting has to be inserted in the row, there's not enough room for the mechanical drill to be used. To facilitate this, a highly advanced piece of B.C. technology in the form of a very large two-handed auger, or *trivella,* with a single helical twist round a solid shank, is called for.

The so-called 'Archimedean screw' was certainly known long before that Greek mathematician demonstrated that a screw system could be adapted, and used for lifting water. His discovery that sitting down in a bath could do it just as well did not, at the time, appear quite as useful. The mark of genius is seeing what others fail to see, and the possibilities of such imagination has always been infinite, even when the advance is only an improvement or an adaption.

There have been many such advances in the vineyard over the last century. Pliny also mentions such drills or augers used by the northern Celtic carpenters and wheelwrights we've met before, but the tool is certainly much older than either. Perfectly round holes bored in the closely compacted sand during construction of 500 B.C. Etruscan tombs in the vicinity of Volterra, demonstrate the possible antecedence of the vineyard *trivella*. The dense, compressed sand is extremely difficult to cut away with a spade or pick, while an auger would have been capable of weakening the surface with less effort by drilling a close line of holes before splitting them out with a pick.

Before this achievement the practice of vegetative propagation appears to have been an early occurrence in the cultivation of vines, as in a wild state they are either self-pollinated or cross-pollinated, resulting in erratic growth and quality. Possibly observing that the trailing branches rooted themselves, early agriculturists at some point perceived the advantage of bringing order to the vines, and assisted superior growth by selected rooting.

The next step, to that of selective grafting, must have been a quantum leap, allowing the cultivator to select the best fruit, and thereby control the quality of the harvest. By the time the first recorded language appeared it seems to have been firmly established. Both these methods are still being used, and a short description follows in this and in an appropriate later chapter.

Etruscans, and later the Romans, used several methods to train their vines, some bearing little in common with the present practice. Being both a climbing and trailing plant they appear, originally, to have grown them simply on trees, notably poplar and elm that have low strong branches, and where the base of the tree was also thick with natural mulch.

Later, they were grown on *Pali*, (*vitus palare*) two sticks stuck in the ground with a cross bar similar to an athletic hurdle. These were fairly low in form, but there are some higher variations, now just as rare.

To gain considerable height a long centre stake with a single cross bar (Latin *jugum*) resembling a Christian cross, on which the vines tendrils were tied with osier or willow twigs, also came to be used.

Small, vividly red or yellow willows - *Salice* (or *Salcio* in Tuscany) - are still seen growing at the end of the vineyard for this purpose, as indeed they are at Sant'Anna. They are not the English 'weeping willow', the large *Salix babylonica*, but the small *Salix viminalis* whose shoots are also commonly used in basketwork.

The vines supported on the small crossbars were cut in the form of a letter 'X' to expose growth to sunlight and air. You may, occasionally, still see ancient *Pali* in the grounds of an abandoned *podere*, though it's not a sight that will long endure. Neither are the basket weavers you now rarely come across in the countryside, tucked away in some small hamlet. Their rustic produce is seemingly too artless for modern use, given they might have lasted for a number of generations.

Pali with cross-poles.

It would possibly be remiss not to mention that, in a similar manner, Etruscans were said to frequently train their vines on very small trees called *testucchi* or *testucchio*, though as the words seem unfamiliar in Latin or Italian they may be colloquial terms for a particular species. Suggestions that *testucchi* might be pergolas or trellises appears a dubious connexion, not being based on any obvious etymological foundation. In Latin *testudo* is a tortoise, and at a stretch its shell might represent a type of canopy, but it seems a flight of fancy.

Vines have long been grown in the form of an arbour, but generally only in a domestic situation where the grapes would be of a variety suitable for the table or as a method of creating shade. This was certainly true in ancient Egypt where vine bowers provided an overarching screen against the fearsome heat of the sun.

As a qualification, such a practice may have derived from an alternative Roman custom of growing vines in the form of a square, as they apparently still do in some parts of Spain, which quite possibly may have naturally formed a bower if of a small area, but that is hardly conclusive.

Given the accumulated evidence from Crete, to Egypt, to the South Caucasus - the true home of *vitis vinifera* from which all modern grapes descend - and also the early Assyrian civilization, where they grew grapes on pomegranate trees, it would appear that viticultural methods were in a constant state of flux. Essentially, as always, farming was dependent on the economic and social conditions of the time.

Classical writers do their very best to confuse the issue. For example, buried in Homer's "Odyssey", Ulysses arrives at the court of Alcinoüs, ruler of Phaeacia, and passes through the palace garden of some four acres, noting: "Here ordered vines in equal ranks appear." As mentioned previously, by the first century A.D., the Romans cultivated their vines in this fashion, but Homer, living in probably the eighth century B.C., seems to suggest the system to be much earlier. However, as the garden he tempts us with appears to be an orchard full of apples, pears, figs, pomegranates and olive trees, it may only turn out to have been a case of poetic licence.

Virgil, author of the 'Georgics', which has much to do with agriculture and its management, was more forthcoming in the later Augustan Age, considering the elm trees he saw in Lombardy an ideal partner for the vine. These were seemingly a dwarf variety that spared the soil while supporting the grateful plant.

On the other hand, Zacharie Mayani in his interesting book 'The Etruscans begin to Speak', makes no reference to any words relating to Etruscan wine or vineyards, which appears odd, as they don't seem to have been such a sober lot according to the Dionysian images occasionally depicted in their art.

Perhaps the last word on this matter should be left to Mrs. Piozzi, better known as Mrs. Thrale, and erstwhile friend of the redoubtable Dr. Samuel Johnson. She had this to say during her journey through Tuscany in the mid 1780's which goes a long way to settling the matter, during that period at least:

'The roadside is indeed hedged with festoons of vines, crawling from olive to olive, which they plant in the ditches of Tuscany as we do willows in Britain: mulberry trees too by the thousand, and some pollarded poplars serve for support to the glorious grapes that will soon now be gathered'.

At this point, with such varied opinion, be it maple, elm, olive, mulberry or poplar, perhaps it is simpler just to accept that one method was to grow them on trees!

To go off on another tangent for a moment, a few words on how the choice of cuttings, and type of grape at Sant'Anna, came to be selected.

It is part of wine folklore that before the turn of the twentieth century the parasitic lice *Phylloxera* attacked the European vines, necessitating the planting of a hardy strain from the United States. What appears not so well known is that there is a strong possibility that *Phylloxera* appeared in Europe on the vines imported from the United States in an effort to mitigate another earlier disease that was having a devastating effect on the growth of vines. If so, by a strange twist of fortune, the cause also turned out to be the cure.

The first of these vine diseases seems to have been noted in the Slater hot-houses of Margate, England, by a Mr. E. Tucker. In 1845 he observed a whitish fungus growing on the vines, later named *'Oidium Tuckeri',* which completely destroyed the fruit. The spores were shortly found in the vineyards of Versailles, and by 1852, had spread over the whole of southern Europe causing wholesale damage to the crops. Sulphur dust was found to be the best remedy, but far from eliminated the disease. At this point, in 1862, Portugal, in desperation, imported Californian vines. By 1863 the disease had abated, but was a prelude to an even greater menace.

Sometime, around 1865, a microscopic insect, *Phylloxera Vastatrix,* had appeared, ravaging the whole of southern Europe, and eventually even appearing in Australia. France, through the administration and research of Pasteur, brought it under control by 1883. In Italy, the disease proved unpredictable, seemingly contained in cooler climates, or where they grew a stronger variety of grape. The robust Nebbiolo grape of Piedmont survived, as did the Blanc de Valdigne of Valle d'Aosta. In Apulia, the legendary Primitivo grape that can reach a huge 18.4°, and is frequently transported to northern Europe as a 'corrective', was destroyed in the zones round Salento in the south; but further north, in the area of Alberobello, survived. The hardy red grape, Refosco del Penduncolo Rosso, remained untouched in Friuli.

In Tuscany; however, the Sangiovese vines were particularly badly devastated, and the decision to introduce a hardy strain of original stock, resistant to the disease in the United States, brings us back to Sant'Anna.

On this *podere*, it was the American type 420/A, which carried the grafted Sangiovese scions on these imported stocks, and what we see today are the ancestors of the original Benini enterprise. The root-stock is generally selected to suit the soil environment - 420/A being suitable for the mineral rich soil found at Sant'Anna. Contrast this with the hotter and dryer south of Italy where the aforementioned Primitivo is often grafted onto the Kober 5BB stock. These type numbers demonstrate the enormous experimentation and analysis of root stock that is still being undertaken in the United States in an effort to combat new grape diseases that constantly appear round the world. It is manifestly a highly specialized and indispensable business when the loss of a season's profits through plant failure can mean bankruptcy, and the inevitable forfeiture of jobs.

Naturally, in fifty years a lot of things can change among the vines, as the vineyard is one of constant regeneration: the constant shuffling by hybridization, planting of experimental varieties, or the necessity of repair in the form of natural propagation, known as *margotta* or *propaggine*. This has led to many hands manipulating the vine growth to suit the moment. Despite this, the vineyard at Sant'Anna remains basically as intended.

In the United Kingdom the practice of natural propagation, familiar to many gardening enthusiasts, is known as 'layering'. Cato gives a detailed explanation in his '*De Agri Cultura*', the oldest extant literary prose work in Latin. The method is still considered the most successful, as while the young plant is making roots, the parent plant continues to provide it with nutrients.

There aren't many farmers of a lazy disposition, but this method would perhaps suit any that are.

In the autumn when a vine has failed in the line at Sant'Anna, the plant is removed, and a convenient trailing branch from an adjacent vine is inserted in a prepared hole and the end bent upwards, leaving the tip above the ground attached to a stake. The hole is then back-filled.

Growth of the new plant may be at risk from cold snaps, so a small pyramid of fine sand provides effective protection from the elements.

Eventually it will produce new shoots - *tralcio.* In the spring it is separated from the main branch, and any buds situated underneath the new stems on this freed branch, are removed. Initially the new plant is kept at approximately 50 centimetres (20 inches) in height to encourage side growth.

In the following year after the initial planting, when some height has been achieved, the most robust and well formed branch on the new vine will be trained to the first wire in a form known as - *cordone orizontale* - a horizontal cordon, or single stem. The rest are removed. In this manner, because it has only one branch, the vine forms what might be described as a truncated espalier, and it may be three years before a successful fruiting takes place.

Ultimately, at the start of the season, with some satisfaction the proprietor can look upon a scene where each cordon in the vineyard points, with beautiful symmetry, in the same direction.

Tuscan vineyard.

The eminent Italian art historian, Giorgio Vasari, may have been slightly confused in supposing that Botticelli was employed in painting frescoes at the Spedaletto in Volterra. *Spedale* is the Tuscan for hospital, and *spedaletto* (-etto being a suffix denoting the diminutive) a small hospital. Volterra certainly has an ancient small hospital of this period, but sadly, no Botticelli. Some of its walls are festooned with a 'Dance Macabre' of skeletons and skulls and crossbones - which seems oppressively sinister for a hospital.

There is; however, another Spedaletto that may have been intended, and credibly indicate the cause of this anomaly. It doesn't really resolve the matter as there isn't a visible Botticelli there either, but as the property once belonged to the Medici during a contemporary period to the artist, it's as probable a place as any other. After all, the Florentine family commissioned frescoes by a local artist, Baldassare Franceschini, known as Volterrano, for the Villa di Castello and the Villa della Petraia overlooking Florence, so it was certainly very much an itinerant occupation among artists during this period. In those days, when the call came, you packed your brushes, and presented yourself - *immediatamente*!

Professor Michael Baxandall in his erudite little book 'Painting and Experience in Fourteenth-Century Italy', reinforces this suggestion of the itinerant artist's location when he makes reference to Botticelli; Filippino Lippi; Perugino and Ghirlandai being recommended by the Duke of Milan's agent 'as they had all worked in the Spedaletto of Lorenzo il Magnifico near Volterra'.

Now, if you have a penchant for walking the dusty white roads, then a pleasant diversion that might help keep you out of a *spedaletto* is to travel along a meandering track the healthy distance between this old Medici *fattoria* called Spedaletto and Sant'Anna.

It's true you may not recall seeing a similar landscape to the one you'd pass through in any of Botticelli's paintings; indeed, such representations that do exist, seem to have a form completely alien to Tuscany. Trees and fanciful rock formations might form part of quattrocento iconography, and the umbrella pine scenes captured in *'La Pineta di Cecina'* are vaguely suggestive, but the artist surely never ambled away his time amongst these hills, or these places.

This is really hardly surprising when you consider that until the emergence of that supreme artist Michelangelo, painters were merely artisans, and expected to labour diligently on a commission, with little time to evaluate the landscape as an autonomous subject.

The contrast between the two sites is emphatic, and will help place Sant'Anna clearly in the economic society existing before the modern world shook the system out of its moribund state.

Spedaletto, being a vast gloomy mixture of monastic, medieval, and later Medici additions, was the hub of a virtually closed world, inhabited by farmers on their podere, stonemasons, carpenters, charcoal makers, and builders with brickworks at their disposal, as well as a host of supplicant workers scattered over the whole domain. All these representative units were tightly coalesced to maintain its existence.

This ponderous mass of buildings defines a vast *azienda agricola*, comprising the traditional Tuscan villa - *fattoria*, with its subservient tenants, and whole vistas to labour over.

Part of a unifying group - Spedaletto, would have been made up of dozens of small *podere*, - while Sant'Anna, is only an example of one of those dozens.

Modern Sant'Anna, in contrast, is not much more than the previously mentioned one hundred acres, visible within the compass of an arm, being in its way the traditional *podere*, - a solitary farmhouse and outbuildings, bound to the *villa-fattoria* - though the small chapel is an unusual feature for a *podere*, indicating a level of independence in a more recent domestic period.

Nevertheless, agricultural practices would have been common to both, sharing as they did, the same resources as well as climate. Grain, olives and grapes would have figured highly in their cultivation. Animals would probably have been kept only for home consumption, enclosed, or tethered nearby during the day.

Commercially, sheep and cattle need enclosed land of considerable acreage, though pigs can forage freely in wooded areas, a tradition still represented by the *Cinta Senese* pigs that are bred in this manner close to Siena, as indeed the Verderer's pigs still are in the New Forest of Hampshire.

The presence of nomadic flocks of sheep in Tuscany seems to have been absent before the middle of the eighteenth century. There appears to have been a very strong prejudice against *pastori*, not least because these shepherds led a wandering life. Appearing in society only intermittently, they generally remained outsiders.

How things have changed. The large villas are still there, either shorn of their acres, and surviving on 'new money', or highly mechanized, relying on as many men as they once relied on whole families. The brickworks are mere ruinous piles with lofty smokeless chimneys, and the once essential *carbonaie*, where the charcoal was stored, are now merely cold, blackened cellars, testimony of a rejected epoch. Today, charcoal is only needed in handfuls for some suburban garden grill, leaving the abandoned *carbonaie* to become silent relics of a slowly disintegrating age.

Yet, conversely, demands on the nation's rural economy ensured that many of the small farms remained small farms, albeit, under a more tolerable private ownership. It is mostly among these that you will find the remnants of the old life, a microcosm that still remains a stubborn detail on the very borders of the present day. In these vineyards you will find elements of the historical work that must be repeated every season, a commitment to the old proficiency where competence was still demonstrated by the hand, and success revealed only by practical results.

Today the art of making wine, at any level, is still founded on creating a tolerable environment, and this means physically coping with the mundane as well as the exotic.

The mature vineyard, left to its own devices, would soon become a nightmare of invading plant life; none of it welcome given it takes the form of a dense cover of ryegrass, cocklebur and pigweed. Benini, to avoid their uninvited company, puts a well-honed strategy into effect just after Christmas.

The ground has been roughly ploughed between the vines during the winter, allowing any ice and frost to helpfully destroy harmful insects and bacteria; then left until the spring, when the disc harrow, or *frangizolle*, is used to break down larger mounds; preparing the soil to a depth of approximately 20 cm (c.8 inches).

This, unfortunately, has the undesirable effect of awakening all the otiose vegetation. Before the end of April the invasion of weeds has become a prolific nuisance, and the area directly beneath the vines, where they lounge in self-assertive insolence, has to be specifically cultivated.

The air becomes heavy with the smell of wild garlic that seems to be particularly excessive in the vicinity of the farmhouse; while miniature clumps of chard further suggest the position might have historically served as a kitchen garden. Now these barbarous ancestors are just a nuisance among the docks and the dandelions. That the milky sap of dock greatly soothes nettle rash might have saved it from persecution, but as there seems a dearth of stinging nettles in this area, that beneficial property is studiously overlooked.

The soil between each stake is incised with a hand held machine - either a strimmer, *decespugliatore*, or if along the rows, a mower, the *tosaerba*, stemming from the word *tosare*, to cut close. In any event, the weeds are cut down and cleared out. However, near to each vine the weeds remain untouched, entailing the need for their removal by hand using the appropriately named *zappa*, or grubbing mattock. In its simplicity it is a truly amazing implement, and it is difficult to see how any gardener in Tuscany could seriously manage without one, as it seems to be their main garden implement.

This supposed Cretan invention, though Neolithic flint examples are numerous, had a diverse history prior to ending up as an implement on the farm. Roman carpenters were particularly fond of an alarmingly constructed twin sided axe-adze, due probably to its labour saving function. It also suggests that if you wanted a plank - first you found your tree!

In comparison to a trying-plane, which uses up a large amount of human energy having no force of its own, the kinetic forces of a falling adze can be minutely adjusted in the hands of an expert to produce a perfectly uniform surface. The single sided adze form is still used by coopers to accurately fashion the staves of casks, and in shipwright's hands up until quite recent times, could be seen fashioning the planks for wooden boats. Surviving in the vineyard its work is less skilful, but conveniently multifunctional.

Francesco Della Cossa, a quattrocento artist from Ferrara, depicts a long purposeful adze resting on a young woman's shoulder as she returns from the vineyard. Entitled *'Allegory of Autumn'* it reminds us of the long connection between the modern implement and the old, immutable nature of agriculture.

Besides removing the weeds, a concave depression can be formed round the vine's base. At the same time the work exposes wasteful feeder roots just below the surface that absorb descending moisture, yet will eventually be burnt by the sun's heat and destroyed. Too fine to be cut off by the adze, for a period of two or three years they are snipped back with secateurs, leaving the deeper roots to strengthen.

The Tuscans have coined a name for this work - *sbarbettatura,* describing the fine beard like hairs that have to be cut - *barba* being the Latin for beard, and where, with a French suffix tacked on to the noun describing a person from the subject of their occupation, becomes the English 'barber'. Nothing like a "short back and sides" to encourage growth.

As the soil on the farm is fairly fertile and productive, little in the way of chemical fertilizer is used, except for a granular plant food added to the bowl to assist the plant's new growth. The granules are a combination of nitrogen, phosphorus, and potassium, and are not reckoned to be specifically organic, but have the advantage of containing the optimum amount of chemical elements necessary for this variety of plant.

Nitrogen and phosphorus are present in all animal organisms, while approximately 120 grams of potassium are present in the average human body, so it actually appears to be as organic as you might wish.

Though there is little evidence that food grown with the help of commercial fertilizers and pesticides has an adverse effect on health, Benini perseveres with his 'minimalist' method, insisting that he is convinced the weather and natural chemistry of the soil will break down an organic product, while a synthetic element will not be so readily dispersed, resulting in oversaturation of the chemical in future plants. The health conscious gastronome would probably tend to agree with him.

It seems then, that the old traditions are not entirely forgotten on these small farms. Organic *concime* - a compost of green manure - is supplied by the roots and stalks of various plants that are high in nitrogen.

Zeno, our stoic philosopher, would have found this type of Benini's 'second legume' more cheering and appetizing than lupin seeds. A bowl of the large table variety in late spring - lightly boiled broad beans, left to cool, then added to onion rings, olive oil and mint, salted and covered in grated *pecorino romano* cheese, is a sure antidote to gastric depression. Along with a coarse fresh bread, and a glass or two of *sfuso*, it would, have provided enough encouragement to beguile those dour ascetics away from their indifference to pleasure. *Baccelli* is the Italian word for pods from which this recipe takes its name, and though it might refer to other legume as well, in this case it is the English broad bean.

Though the small broad beans (also edible) used for compost, known as *favetta* or *Favino Romano,* can be planted in autumn or spring, and harvested six months later, to be of immediate use to the vines, a field of the bean is planted in November. After the beans have been harvested, the plant is cut down, and the roots dug up. The ancient Greeks ploughed the remaining plant straight into the soil, but for residual fruit like the grape the practice is to have them crushed and ground before being ploughed into the lanes between the vines.

A little animal manure comes gratis, courtesy of the wild boar. These fellows are nothing like a nice pink Tamworth, nor quite as gruesome as a Warthog, but they're big bruisers with hides visually reminiscent to the skin of a black gooseberry, and best given a wide berth.

Attentive, as they always were in agricultural matters, the Romans, and later the Italians, sourced the fertilizers for their vines from a variety of animals, using dove as well as heavier farmyard manure. The former was particularly abundant when many country dwellings had a dovecote as part of their animal husbandry. White, wild doves, smaller than pigeons, and not scavengers like their cousins, are still numerous in the area of Sant'Anna, though they are no longer kept domestically, to supplement the produce available for the kitchen.

The original practice, and indeed the architectural style such appendages formed, lived on into the first half of the twentieth century. Their remains, scattered over the countryside of Tuscany, can still be observed in large attractive, angular shaped farmhouses, with a substantial lantern set squarely on top.

In January or February, depending on the weather, attention must be immediately turned to hard pruning.

At this stage, last year's now leafless growth, is still present, high above its black twisted progenitor that barely reaches the first wire.

Looking at the tangled mesh of branches, the words of Benini are lost on uncomprehending grey matter. "What we need are few eyes - *occhi* - for many branches."

Its meaning, given the thousands of branches visible, was not at all clear, until more inspirational advice followed.

Benini is in fact talking about the new buds, or 'eyes', from which the many branches will ultimately appear. Briefly, it can be summarized as determining which wood is to be removed; which branch will form the best cradle for growth; avoid disorderly crowding and confusion, and allow a productive spread of new branches to take place. Not quite a nod towards Darwin's natural selection.

Therefore, they have to be cut off.

Two thousand vines, depicting the sheer scale of the work that needs to be accomplished, and this on a relatively small farm.

Benini added a caveat. A few eyes - those beautiful tufts that will sprout everywhere - meant two eyes. Precisely, that is, on every branch. As most will soon have half a dozen buds, or more, it's fairly easy to grasp his point.

Branches are to be seen as conduits dispersing life giving sugars, hormones and mineral elements carried in the sap. 'The more the merrier' is not seen as a good thing, being like a surprise guest at a dinner party, with the need to make a 'small loaf' go a great deal further. For this reason, it is just as well to remember, that up is where everything, eventually, is supposed to be going.

As ninety percent of the branches completely ignore this criteria, it is apparent that what is about to take place will be a viticultural massacre.

This is probably one of the reasons why Benini jumped at the chance of an extra pair of hands!

To make his point, he reiterates: the aim is to clear the vine of this woven network of last year's branches, and may be determined - indeed is invariably determined - by leaving only two, perhaps three, *razzole*, or cut branches, remaining on the old vine. On these will be left two undeveloped new buds, or eyes, pointing in the right direction.

Hence the first part of Benini's expression: 'few eyes'. Two seems little enough. The 'many branches', is a reference to the new progeny that will quickly cluster on the rapid growth of these originally chosen shoots, and will have to be trained to branch along the stretched wires.

Trained branches.

Benini takes the measure of all this activity by the winds. The dry, cold *Tramontana* will stay his hand, as the severed branch would be cruelly exposed to its still bitter blast. This wind can be leisurely or incredibly violent, and not one that the farmer ever takes for granted. Local legend argues that a *Tramontana*, emanating from Siberia, will last for one, three or five days, and if there is any truth in the matter, a few days delay won't be of much account. A little later the cold and humid *Grecale* can be just as destructive, freezing the new tufted shoots that begin to form in spring. Everything in the vineyard seems to be a gamble.

The pruning normally takes place on last year's new wood. It sometimes happens, where the old has become so badly positioned, that another 'older' branch has been trained from the year before to take its place. When the time comes, the misaligned mature wood can also be cut back. It must be added, that though this may be the exception rather than the rule, the occasion is entirely dependent on the experience of the pruner.

In any case, there is no question of just paring away the branches. The body language of a novice pruner sums up the responsibility that has suddenly descended upon their shoulders. They will stand deep in thought before a vine, with all the air of a chess champion, summing up the next move. Such deliberation is curiously physical, body moving one way, then the other before a branch is sacrificed. More contemplation followed by a tentative step prior to another commitment.

Benini is already six vines further along. He doesn't mind. If at the end of the morning his acolyte has managed two rows, they will represent two less he will have to manage. Like all good farmers, sanguine and economical, he has learnt to be tolerant of clumsy, but willing, hands.

Such merciless extirpation must have fostered a barbarous side to the pruner's character. Robert Graves, poet, author and classical scholar, grimly informs us that the vinedressers of Syria and Asia Minor had a custom of seizing and killing passing strangers during the vintage season. Similar harvest sacrifices were known to have taken place all over Europe. Heracles - a gentleman of prodigious strength - is credited with its abolition, and though animals figure strongly in his efforts, none of his twelve great tasks, or 'labours', seems to have included pruning a vineyard. There is some mention of harrowing hell, but it seems likely that only E.U. officials would look for a vineyard there!

Viti selvatiche, wild vines thrown out from a sucker on the original root stock, with spindly maroon coloured branches too thin to hold themselves erect, sprawl out in a tangle from under the domestic growth where they are invariably uprooted and discarded as parasitic.

Very occasionally; however, a sturdy example of the

wild vine can serve for propagation if new growth is to be encouraged, and layering is not an immediate possibility. As the pruning takes place, little ribbons in a bright material tied round a branch, flags that it has been selected as a scion for the purpose of grafting. The exposed vascular tissue of the scion is then matched to the tissue of the cut wild stock, bound in, given a protective covering, usually tar, and two to three weeks later with a modicum of luck, a new generation has established itself.

Without scientific knowledge of genetic cultivars at Sant'Anna, this practice must be carefully controlled once the plant bears fruit for signs of reversion, producing a less juicy, perhaps more acidic, grape.

As soon as the first visible growth appears - flecks of green unfolding buds - great care is taken in controlling the moulds that attack the vines, and recalling its historical destruction of grapes, it is hardly surprising that farmers are paranoiac about the possibility of a recurrence. None can afford to lose too high a percentage of the harvest; one of the complications encountered by organic growers.

Treatment is restricted to fungicide; sulphur for various moulds during April, and a mixture of *poltiglia bordolese*, copper and lime, used in the summer after a downpour, when the combination of rain and sun is at its most destructive. The humidity can then be seen rising in a vaporous mist round the leaves and skin of the young grapes, so that the whole vineyard resembles a verdurous Turkish bath.

This activity can become a relentless exercise; a war of attrition against one of the downsides of nature, for having sprayed the vines any new fall of rain will wash away the protection, and the process will have to be repeated all over again.

The success of the year's harvest will depend on Benini's constant vigilance, and on any day from the onset of spring you will see his solitary figure walking among the vines, peering attentively at the foliage.

In the early part of the year he will be particularly preoccupied. His normally beaming face takes on a serious frown, his lips pressed tight in apprehension as he lifts the minute, developing grapes into the light, for this is the time when Mister Tucker's grey mould - *muffa grigia* - is prevalent. The faintest hint, and the plant must be sprayed with a mixture of sulphur and water, or *oidium* and water, leaving behind a yellow tint on the vines.

Thereafter, two times a month, the bowser is pulled up and down the avenues, spraying the crops with a mixture of copper, sulphur and water to control the ever present chance of *peronospora della vite* - mildew. You will know it's been done, leaving behind the ubiquitous blue stain to puzzle the uninitiated. You will also know when it hasn't by the dark brown, wizened grapes that crumble to dust when you touch them.

Some organic horticulturists maintain that milk is a preventative for some mildew, but on a commercial scale appears an impracticable remedy.

As they both seem to be fungal by nature, and being innocent of knowledge where these matters are concerned, you might well ask: what is the difference between a mould and a mildew?

"Now listen carefully," Benini explained. "The mould is *Botrytis cinerea*. The mildew is *Uncinula necator. Va bene*?"

Right! Ask a silly question...

Moving oneself swiftly on to safer ground, he was more forthcoming on another question that generally puzzles those who are visiting a vineyard. As you travel around the Tuscan countryside, and no doubt in other regions as well, you may come across a rose bush planted at the end of one of the lines of vines. Once by no means common, in recent years the practice seems to have become more widespread. There doesn't appear to be any preference for a particular variety, though red or white coloured roses predominate. That they enhance the romanticism of the inspirational Tuscan countryside goes without saying.

However, it seems that they aren't planted in any flight of fancy, for having a similar growth pattern to a vine they perform a quite different, though supportive, role.

Despite the delicate, sensual appearance of the flower, rose plants are extremely hardy. This is no bad thing given Tuscan winters, yet the emerging buds are more fragile than those of the vine, and more readily attacked by mould. In this they are then presumed to act as an alarm bell, an early warning system to spray the vines before they are also beset by the affliction.

Not that the benefit from this harmonious, and mostly fragrant plant, are said to end there. The argument seems to be that roses in the vineyard have yet another virtue. They are said to produce a chemical that repels aphids and white fly, a pest that afflicts grapes in some areas, and that roses can transfer this chemical benefit to vines. The only downside to this attractive solution is that roses are badly affected by these insects themselves. Gardeners will readily recommend battalions of ladybirds rather than roses.

It has also been suggested that the nasturtium can be an equally effective deterrent, but so far this plant, as far as one can see, has not yet made an appearance among the vines!

Yet despite these attractive novelties there may be a historical precedent to the original point of this account, as during the ancient dynastic period of Ramses III, when taxes were collected in the form of agricultural produce rather than money, Egyptian hieroglyphic records indicated that they imported both vines and roses from Anatolia. It is not known whether they suffered from white fly and aphids or not, but on the strength of an obvious desire to offset the failure of crops to service this onerous contribution, you might well be tempted to argue, that there's nothing new under the sun.

Towards the end of May, when Tuscany has taken on a landscape clothed in swathes of emerald and jade more in common with Sussex and the South Downs of England than Italy, the vine has almost doubled in height. It is a shockingly spirited grower, and the first stage of organizing these new, unruly offspring colonizing the spaces of those that have been cut away only a few months before, presses strongly on Benini's time. The aim now, he articulates pointedly, is to optimize the growth and quality of the grapes, besides facilitating the arduous task of picking them. The cutting and trimming is a process that will continue until the grapes are well formed in July.

The leading shoot - *arricciamento delle foglie* - is trained so that its growth will be directed strongly along the wire. Luckily, the first word has been pared down from its root, *riccio* to *cirro* - 'curly' in this particular case, not as in its other meaning, that of a 'hedgehog', though as this little quadruped can curl itself up into a ball, it is also valid in this respect. The result, regardless, will be leaves that are the largest on the vine; huge green parasols offering abundant, but not obfuscating shade to the grapes clustering beneath.

All this activity has taken place on the black stump of old wood, which if you hadn't known, had all the appearance of nothing more useful than material for the bonfire, or indeed, had already been in some inferno.

On the trailing branch, the two shoots referred to as *occhi* - eyes - that have been encouraged, one on each side, one high and one low, will have begun to make their own contribution. The only problem in attending to their progress is that the human eyes develop a divergent squint by the end of the day.

The reason for the pedantic pruning activity is now about to become obvious. The branches they have fostered also have *occhi*, and depending on how long it has been since their last inspection, may well be festooned with these beautiful silver and rose coloured tufts. They are everywhere, sprouting in such burgeoning profusion that left to their own design you can imagine what will happen. Only so much nourishment can be drawn out of the soil to feed this frenetic proliferation.

Something has to be done about it.

Back to the trusty secateurs, and not feeling in the least bit like Smollett's trusty Humphry Clinker - a powerful labourer in the Lord's vineyard. (Not an insignificant allusion, as Smollett lies interred in Livorno's *'Antico Cemitero Inglesi'* - the English cemetery in the Via Verdi.)

Two secondary shoots, selected in the same manner as the initial pruning, have their stems cut off above these newly chosen *occhi*, terminating their growth.

As in everything to do with nature, there must be exceptions to the rule. A particularly good stem - capable of filling a gap between the vines for instance - will be left to grow with only a pinching out of its mass of tufts. The aim, despite this departure from the norm, is to keep no more than four *occhi* on the two newly selected branches. As such, they represent the optimum foundation at Sant'Anna for a harvest of acceptable quality. Benini would like to grow less grapes to achieve a higher quality - two *occhi* for instance, one on each branch - but that would mean less wine per vine at the end of the day, with only the planting of more vines to make up the deficit. Sadly, that spoilsport Domitian, and his modern accomplices, still cast a long shadow over such an idea.

Besides, there are enough tears already. It is quite remarkable how much liquid is coursing through the stem of a plant. When a necessary trimming is made the cut branch emits a steady trickle of liquid, referred to as *la vite piange* - the vine weeps. It has a slightly pithy taste, won't give you a headache, and a sure sign that the vineyard is well into spring.

The independent Tuscans call *grappolo*, the productive pale green cluster of berries, *ciocca*, probably in reference to their slender tips that have a similarity, at one stage, to a lock of hair.

From May to July, stems that do not carry any bunches of the tiny grapes referred to as *grappolo*, are selectively removed. These large leaved, fruitless side shoots, are referred to as *femminelle*.

Though surprisingly prolific and vigorous, appearing at an insistent and alarming rate in all directions, *femminelle* are not in the least fertile, despite the inference of the name. Admittedly, they could be said to resemble a vegetal Amazon. Regrettably, as they absorb large quantities of precious moisture to no effect, they are relentlessly pursued and eliminated. Along with their quasi-parasitic existence, the abundance of their leaves will completely obscure the developing bunches of grapes from the sun. They also effectively deny the fruit receiving any deterrent against disease during the necessary spraying periods.

Grappolo.

To match all this vigorous proliferation in the vineyard there can be no respite. The work will take two people about an hour to clear a row of vines, as like a carpenter, one speedily develops the habit of measuring twice, and cutting once. With the occasional Benini good - natured roar of 'Madonna!' at his acolyte's indiscretion, it takes a contemplative week to complete the vineyard.

If the weather is humid, growth will have been so considerable that almost as soon as the work is finished, must begin again like a Sisyphean punishment. Rain in May and June, followed by a hot sun overhead, plus the soles of stout boots chock-a-block with clinging clay, makes this an arduous task. It's like constantly trying to stop water draining from a colander; cutting, training, alert to the presence of mould, spraying, digging out any stray weeds just about to settle in, worrying about any change in the weather and yet, still many months away from nature's verdict, where everything can be right - and just as easily be wrong.

By late June the grape clusters begin to swell, and take on their recognizable form. Each stem is carried on one of the three wires, with the centre tending to carry the heaviest growth. To restrain its tendency to sag, or belly out, two lines of string run either side of the wire in an attempt to constrain the stem from flopping over. Occasionally the weight is so great that even this is not enough, and the two pieces of string are tethered together by another piece linked between them. Yet one more example of the very Heath-Robinson solutions resorted to by Tuscan farmers of the 'old school'.

The tremendous strain created by this solid wall of leaves reveals another uncertainty. If the sun and rain are essential ingredients to the growth of the vine, no such benefits seem to be accrued from the wind. A mild breeze would dry the vines, it's true, but Tuscany seems to get more than its fair share of draughts, nearly always at untimely moments. In July, high winds smashing against the billowing sail of leaves will find any weakness in the old posts that looked serviceable only months before, bringing down a section of the row with its shattered mast. It is repaired in-situ, jury-rigged at the expense of bruised grapes and leaves.

To obtain some idea on the scale and growth of a grape-vine an extraordinary example of its power and enormous bulk came to be demonstrated in the most unlikely of places. A grape-vine planted in the United Kingdom at Hampton Court, grew to a length of 36 metres (120 feet) and a height of 7 metres (23 feet); producing in 1910 an extraordinary 2272 bunches of grapes. The greatest recorded weight of grapes, in 2001, was 3893 kilograms (8.44 *quintali*) enough it would appear, if they weren't dessert grapes, to produce 900 litres of wine. The stem of this vine had a diameter of 1.273 metres (4.18) feet). This appears to be a world record, and one supposes it took a little more than some wire and bamboo canes to hold it up, besides keeping it well out of the draught!

During this part of the season the wind may be an unwelcome visitor, but it isn't the only subversive trespasser amongst the vines. No visible benefit, except perhaps at the table, can be attributed to the pheasants who can happily munch their way through low hanging bunches of grapes, generally the white Malvasia. The wild boar, equally of a voracious appetite, at least leaves that small payment of manure, which might pass as a kind of quid pro quo. Craftily, both their activities are generally restricted to the end clusters, as their native instinct guards them against the enclosed avenues of vines through which they would find it difficult to show a clean pair of heels

Despite this frustration, all the farmer can do is contemplate that their reckoning is long past the eleventh hour, and patiently wait for their comeuppance when the hunting season arrives in the autumn. However, this event doesn't get into its stride until well after the end of the harvest. Only then will some of these destructive and tasty guests find their license has finally expired.

X: To Be or Not to Be

Given the giddy pheasant's preference for white grapes; seemingly almost exclusively that of Malvasia at Sant'Anna, and given the grape's paramount importance in the making of its wine, they naturally deserve more than a small measure of attention. The anomaly of a 'sweet toothed' bird shouldn't; however, distract us from what appears a supporting role for red grapes.

Benini cultivates white and red grapes, though with 60% of the grapes being white, these frivolous 'scrumpers' appear to be pampered.

The paucity of red grapes might indicate an original intention to produce a surfeit of refreshing white wine rather than a generic Chianti. If the local climate was warmer on average during the middle of the last century before settling into its more recent periodic spell of cooler weather, then perhaps Benini's father had an intuitive instinct on how things would be in his lifetime.

Malvasia grapes

Surprisingly, in nature there are no 'white' grapes as wild grapes are always red, and any white grapes that appear are albino mutations. Their establishment as a specific variety can be put down to man's persistent experiments to improve the stock. In Tuscany, botanists established that Colorino, frequently used to deepen the colour of a wine, and Canaiolo, both red and white grapes used in Carmignano (a favourite of the renaissance physician and poet Redi, who had an aversion to water, given the temper of one of his poems), are both direct descendents from wild vines.

But, there have also been other changes influencing our appreciation of wine. The evidence quietly amassed by scientific research has tended to favour the beneficial aspects of red wine over white, and whether this is true or not, as the information percolates down through media interest, it may well lead to a change in the public's taste. The present perception, added to this narrowing culture, emphasises that 'mixing your drinks' creates a physically negative effect. Such opinions can't have helped. Whatever the cause, there seems to have been a swing change in societies preferences.

Though there is no statistical evidence to the contrary, red table wine, *sfuso* included, from an observational point of view does appear to have become more popular in Tuscany. Spumante, always appreciated by Italians, still serves as the ultimate applause to the final course, and though dry white versions commonly called Prosecco are increasingly popular, would not necessarily be considered a table wine, though the alcoholic strength does not exclude it.

Benini, while resolutely consuming his white wine, is disappointed at the imbalance created by the preference given to the planting of the initial grape variety. Historically, that decision in some way may have been influenced by memories of weakness in the Sangiovese stock. A willingness to change course now on so small an acreage, coupled to legal restraints, would take a decade to make any real impression. So things are fated to remain as they are.

Though not a recognized zone, and without any classification, the area in which Sant'Anna is situated finds itself cradled by the Chianti Colline Pisane and the Chianti Colli Senesi. These are two districts of designated Chianti producers east and west of Volterra. Geographically, this should allow those farmers with the inclination, to produce a respectable wine.

Certainly, the results achieved should not be

compared to the red wines of ancient Etruscan Veii on the outskirts of Rome - of so poor a quality that it wasn't allowed to be drunk on festive occasions. The venerable sommelier, it seems, could be just as fastidious as the modern one.

Horace; however, a veritable Hugh Johnson of his day, chose to dispute this aspersion, and as he was no mean toper, we can take it as read that he turned a leery eye on the sort of negative criticism that was probably based on a poor year, or the 'sour grapes' (pun intended) of some Roman pedant.

Not that such criticism has ever had any real influence on the makers of *sfuso*, though the immediate area that encompasses Sant'Anna cannot be said to be over endowed with vineyards, while almost suffocated with them on every side. It is probable that the answer to the scarcity of commercial wine in the area of Volterra lies elsewhere.

Now, this is not to say that there is little wine, just that it doesn't bear comparison with the density of wine produced by its neighbour, San Gimignano, for example. Neither does it indicate that its wine would be of a lesser quality. Historically, it is recorded, that Uguccione della Faggiula in his war against the Guelphs, 'ravaged the valuable vineyards of Volterra and lay waste the lands of Pistoja and San Miniato.'

One of the compensations for this supposed neglect is that as olive trees flourish best on land with good drainage, then a hilly sandy, rocky terrain such as this, probably favours their produce over grapes, and the olive oil produced in the zone round Volterra is certainly of a very high quality. This may have restricted the planting of vines, besides the not to be overlooked fact, that wine is also more labour intensive to produce, with its consequent need for a stable population in constant attendance.

The economics of olive oil and wine are; nevertheless, equally precarious, both being very dependent on the weather, with the need to fine-tune the growth of their fruit. The bottom line seems to be that one never hears of a glut in olive oil that, in its cold pressed form, is consistently expensive. This is no surprise when an olive tree might supply just three litres of oil, more often less. Grapes, on the other hand, unless the season is exceptionally unfavourable, supply a high percentage of wine.

On top of this, wine is almost always pressed by the producer, while olives, unless from a very large *azienda*, have to be transported to a *frantoio*, or commercial oil pressing mill. Not a lot of chance for price elasticity there!

Despite this, given the right conditions, some wine producers in the area have applied themselves to create commercial viability out of their vines, though it's taken dedication, and a willingness to make considerable investments. As such, they have become the antitheses of the concept surrounding *sfuso* made on the small Italian farm. (The existence of Estate *sfuso* is touched on briefly, later in the chapter.)

In any case, the soil can't be totally blamed for this neglect, as the Romans demonstrated the possibilities with poor sites in far more hostile conditions than that found in the Val d'Era.

The quality of the terrain surrounding Volterra is of a different dimension, and for a fair comparison is somewhat similar to the countryside south of Siena, trapped between Montalcino and Montepulciano. Bleaker, but starkly similar in winter, the land is bleached white by the wind that manages it seems, to suck the very moisture out of the stones. Sangiovese may be grown in those zones, but then, it isn't a recognized district for Chianti either.

Having permitted commercial viticulture to mostly lapse in the immediate area of Volterra (the small but successful Montescudaio *consorzio* rubs shoulders with it in the west, close to Cecina), and with mechanization and technology promoting the much more secure economical enterprise of grain production, there is probably little chance of a general revival. That leaves small *podere* like Sant'Anna to maintain an ancestral tradition, which regrettably, will also soon be gone.

For the moment, though by no means to be considered as such, the red wine of Sant'Anna conforms to the archetypal Chianti.

There can be little doubt that even in the appropriate zones, Chianti has varied considerably over the centuries. It's not even known if the wine was always called Chianti, for the type was shipped to London during the Middle Ages where it was described as Florence Red, or simply Florence, a name that persisted well into the nineteenth century. This would seem to indicate that the export of Chianti commenced in Florence and only later came to be applied to other zones; possibly when Tuscany became a duchy under the Medici. In this, some commentators consider Chianti may well have been the world's first dry red wine, though the variety of grape remains undecided.

The grapes known to have been used in Tuscany during medieval times, were Trebbiano and Vernaccia for white wine, while for the red, Vermiglio, a grape that seems no longer to exist. Whether the latter's name is in reference to the colour vermilion, a vivid red, is only speculation. It is worth noting that Italy has identified over two thousand grape varieties existing on the peninsula, with no doubt many more that have passed into oblivion. Speculatively, such an early wine may have born some resemblance to a Sangiovese corrected with the contemporary vivid Colorino grape.

At least one hint of a formula has surfaced, that of Baron Bettino Ricasoli, who in the late nineteenth century was said to have declared that his Chianti '*sfuso*' was a blend of Sangiovese, Canaiolo, and occasionally a small amount of Malvasia. One can almost guarantee that opened a can of worms!

At this point, it is just as well to reiterate that *sfuso, per se*, is not Chianti, being any grape variety from any region, white or red, produced and intended to be drunk within the year following the *vendemmia*. For this reason, it is probable that all vineyards, from the exiguous to the enormous, tend to produce *sfuso*.

Chianti is a style of wine quintessentially Tuscan and; therefore, as the predominant grape variety in the region is Sangiovese - the essential component in Chianti - it is hardly surprising that most local vineyards produce something of the same nature. But they are not necessarily Chianti, which must be produced in seven defined zones, of which Classico, lying between Florence and Siena, is the most famous. (See appendix.)

There is no pedantic formula that a *podere* chooses to follow. Their wine will depend very much on the quantity, and type of grapes to hand, which may bear some relation to the legal definition of Chianti. Not least, and this is very much a determining factor, the geographical limits of the vineyard may well resolve a particular title, but only if it conforms to the *consortium*, or *consorzio* rules for that zone. There is no compulsion for a producer within the Chianti zones to belong to a *consorzio* unless it intends to use the name Chianti, and all vineyards; therefore, can produce *sfuso* if they choose.

For this reason, the wine of Sant'Anna provides a natural contrast between the style of wine an independent *podere* might create, and the government regulations that control the use of the title Chianti.

A brief description of the regulations (which in reality are both lengthy and complicated) for the making of Chianti, will present a good example of what percentage of grapes, in one form or another, might go into a *podere sfuso* as well. Despite this, it still won't be Chianti.

Since 1996, Chianti Classico (that of the Black Cockerel label - the Gallo Nero) has had its own set of much stricter regulations, including colour and scent, which has radically altered the character:

Chianti (old regulations):			Sant'Anna:
Red:	Sangiovese	50/70%	60%
	Canaiolo	10/30%	10%
White:	Trebbiano	10/30%	20%
	Malvasia	10/30%	10%

(From this it can be seen that Sant'Anna conforms to the old regulations for Chianti. When the comparison is with the new rules for Chianti; however, it no longer meets those requirements.)

Chianti (new regulations):
Red Sangiovese 80-100%.
(If not 100% then the other 20% must be red grapes from a delimited, or designated, area within the Chianti zone. Since 2006 no white grape has been permitted.
Chianti Classico has additional requirements of a minimum alcohol content of 12%, with seven months in wood. For a Riserva, twenty-four months, including bottle ageing, before release.)

As there is a permanent flux in the drawing up of rules to accommodate new marketing influences the above brief specifications are not guaranteed to be extant at the time of this books publication.

Obviously a great deal of variation may be produced in the old style of the wine, and intentionally, a very much more restricted product in the new regulations for Chianti Classico. The absence of white grapes has allowed for a much fuller bodied wine, more in line with modern commercial practice.

That is not something that will be commonly shared with a small *podere*, who would sensibly eschew pulling out all their white grapes for the sake of fashion. Being such individualists they have never much cared for *consortium* rules anyway. That is not to say that a particular *podere* will not produce a traditional generic style of Chianti, or a one hundred percent Sangiovese *sfuso*. Many choose to do so, with considerable variations in between.

Where the *podere* is concerned, a greater interpretation of style than that afforded by the *consorzio* is possible by what is known colloquially as *corretto*, a correction determined by the legally defined *'governo all'uso toscano'*.

The now defunct minimum alcoholic strength for Chianti was 11.5°, that for Classico 12°, and Riserva 12.5°. In poor years many estates would have struggled to reach these figures, and a permitted correction under the *consortium* rules was introduced. That is, a percentage of wine - or more often 'must' - with a higher alcohol grade could be added. This was deemed a necessary commercial practice; one widely used wherever grapes were grown in Italy to add body and taste.

Be aware that where a *podere sfuso* is concerned, the legally defined 'this or that' is not worth a fig. Its character, or strength, hangs on the whims of the maker, its only success on whether it is an acceptable beverage or not!

Perversely, the *corretto* was never a universal practice in Tuscany. *Governo*, - the shortened name for the regulations on the use of the 'must' from semi-dried grapes to be described more fully shortly - was not permitted in Vino Nobile di Montepulciano, for example.

We digress. For Chianti, the correction carried out in the vineyard used to be 5 - 10 percent, (15 percent according to some authorities) of the grapes picked during the year prior to the *vendemmia*, and semi-dried on *canniccio*, a type of cane mat. As early as the fourteenth century, documents indicate that grapes had been set aside to dry, so the resulting very strong wine from these dried grapes could be added to new wine, inducing or elevating a second fermentation.

This practice of correcting the standard wine with a

percentage sourced from raisins may be one of those ancient skills passed down to us, as both raisins and wine were known in the Bronze Age, c.3000 B.C.

A more recent alternative has been to use the 'must' of a strong wine from southern Italy, a partially dehydrated concentrate of the skins, stems and seeds of the grapes, but there has also evolved a tendency among commercial vineyards to grow grapes locally, generally Cabernet and Merlot. Even so, as the weather is anything but reliable in Italy this far north, it is considered politic to keep a little of a southern 'must' variety, either syrup or cake, in reserve.

The *corretto* provides an interesting story of its own. Somewhere during this early viticultural process a clever soul fiddling with the manufacture of raisins perfected a system that produced one of the great wines of Italy. What, you may ask, has one of the great wines of Italy got to do with our plebeian *sfuso*? Not so much these days it's true, but once, considerably more.

Recioto della Valpolicella, which is quite a mouthful, metaphorically as well as categorically, seems to have been born out of this method of correction. It's made a long way from Tuscany, above Verona, near Lake Garda. Recioto is a reference to a process employed to produce a type of wine of which Amarone can be regarded as the most famous.

Many will be familiar with Valpolicella, a light bodied, but fruity red wine of probably ancient origin. It carries the name of an area that has thus given its name to the grape. The grapes used, and the percentages, are specific, but extremely variable, somewhat in the manner of Chianti. From a selection of these Valpolicella grapes, Amarone is produced. If you apply the *recioto* process to them, it produces a big, dry and powerfully concentrated wine, which with some ageing demonstrates huge complexity. Indeed, providing the sort of wine that takes a whole evening to contemplate.

Such a mature wine has been described as having the characteristics of a fine Armagnac. When made by the top producers such as Masi or Allegrini, this is a fair description of its bouquet. In the same manner that you can imagine the scent of violets in Chianti Classico, that for Amarone are roses, almonds or violets, depending on the district. Almonds being the most prized, and perhaps because of the astringent under taste that is part of its character, *amaro* (bitter) might be considered an attribute of its name. As you might expect, an Amarone *sfuso* is; therefore, something to write home about, especially as its cost can set you back as much as a reasonable appellation wine.

So what has this got to do with the local *sfuso*? As implied previously, not much nowadays, but rather more with the old and time-consuming method used to produce the concentrated grapes needed to increase the alcoholic strength for a correction.

The grapes from the *vendemmia* selected for this process are usually harvested late in September, and spread out on the open work cane trays or mats (occasionally in Tuscany called *grattici* instead of *canniccio*). Sometimes, the grapes selected may have been those at the top part of the vine, left behind to ripen further in the sun - hence the name *recioto* is supposed to have derived from the colloquial word *recia*, meaning ear. The grapes stay for approximately six months on these trays, so the moisture can evaporate allowing the sugar to concentrate; then they are crushed, followed by a slow fermentation of between four to six weeks. Once the wine has settled, it is moved to wooden casks for the secondary fermentation, and stored in the *cantina* until the next year's *vendemmia*. In this state it can reach 17° alcohol. There you also have the necessary classical correction for a less than robust *sfuso*.

In case you consider such a method produces a type of Amarone, you'd be disappointed.

Beside the magic of the oenologist - those who practice the black arts of wine making - Amarone is then aged in oak barrels for between four and six years. Some producers keep it longer. On the other hand, there are those who believe that with Amarone, the producer should aim for balance, and that does not always necessarily come with long barrel ageing. Nevertheless, it follows that this is a costly wine to make, and justifiably expensive. The end product of this method is an exclusive consumable appellation wine, and not to be confused with wine destined to be used as a correction.

Time is the critical factor, and as they say in business: 'time is money'.

Those who are familiar with Homer's Odyssey will surely not have forgotten Ulysses' son, Telemachus, arriving at Pylos in his search for his father, and hearing the welcoming utterances of Nestor:

Of social welcome, mix'd the racy wine
(Late from the mellowing cask restored to light,
By ten long years refined, and rosy bright.)

Ten years! For an Amarone certainly, but for Benini's purpose, such longevity would have been of no interest. On a small *podere* it is not likely that many farmers could find the time to indulge in such sophistication, even to produce a standard correction. This process was always applied to the next year's wine. However, those farmers that can find the time and interest, are more likely to produce a Vin Santo for festive occasions, which only takes a minimum of three years!

Benini remembers his father producing such a *corretto*, but even so, it really was merely to provide that swift addition of the year old grape juice to the new, following the chemist's analysis of the wine in that period before commercial musts were available. The semi-dried grapes used for *sfuso* correction simply wouldn't have such expensive time and attention spent on them today when a much speedier and convenient correction is available.

Not all grapes would have been suitable for a *sfuso* correction. The slow maturing, much vaunted Cabernet mentioned earlier, would never have been an ideal choice for a wine that needed to be ready for drinking as soon as possible, and it is doubtful that any small *podere* would have introduced such an initially discordant grape for this reason. If such a blending is found available as *sfuso*, it will likely represent surplus wine from a *vendemmia* normally committed to wooden barrels - an Estate *sfuso* in fact.

If you do come across such a wine you are hardly likely to miss it as it has a very dark plum colour with a pronounced fruity taste allied to a very acidic dryness. However, it is a rare *sfuso* amongst its kind, that left for two, even three years in bottles, will have lost a large percentage of its sharpness, and become very much more approachable and interesting; albeit, still a *sfuso* type.

Pliny, very much on his home patch between the River Po and the Alps, describes a method similar to *recioto* observed during his perambulations, which leads us to suppose that even in his day, long before medieval times, it was a tried and tested process.

The outcome of this evolution, gradually led to the change in the *consortium* rules for Chianti, reflected in the specific use of 'other' grapes, with those for Classico grown locally.

These developments have had a knock-on effect too. Some skilful makers of *sfuso* were not slow to notice the pronounced similarity between Sangiovese and Montepulciano d'Abruzzo, a much stronger grape having affinity with the Sangiovese clones: Prugnolo, Gentile and Brunello, which produce world class wines. In combination they make a smoother style of *sfuso*, though still robust, and because the Montepulciano may carry the genes of Sangiovese, might well be truly termed genuine. However, 'authentic' would be a better word in English, as the Italian word *genuino*, in reference to wine, has a slightly different sense. Albeit, a word you will often hear in reference to *sfuso*. Not necessarily meaning a good, or superior wine, but a compliment to one that has been honestly made; therefore, will be natural, pure, and available at a moderate price.

As an old Tuscan proverb reminds us, *sfuso* is expected to fit into the rhythm of local life:

'Pane di un giorno - Vino di un anno.'
'Bread of one day - Wine of one year.'

Given so short a life, a good *sfuso* has to reach the correct balance in an equally short time. A lucky union of grape varieties is a bounty indeed. At Sant'Anna, Benini points out, for the purpose of raising the level of sugar they have planted some rows of Merlot Noir, the sugary red claret grape, rather susceptible to mould in poor years, and Barbera, a normally astringent red grape, though sweet varieties are found in Piedmont which has become its natural home. Within the possibilities of such composites it seems hardly credible there is any recognizable local style of wine at all, or that any statement about grapes or wine can be valid in a holistic sense. Barbera, like Cabernet, has detractors when cited as a good choice for the *governo*, having, according to them, a reputation for a nose like an aged Pirelli tyre, forcing the Piedmontese wine producers to first soak it in oak.

Barbera, let it be said, can be quite excellent; at its

best when young, and quite capable of making a perfectly agreeable *sfuso*. Having noted that reputations are sometimes ill deserved, Genovese *trattorie* in Liguria are known to sometimes be a source for those who want to prove a point. However, Barbera is grown in four zones in Piedmont, and each with a subtly different character, so it pays to take note which zone the wine originated from.

The supposed slight trace of Iris in the aroma of Chianti (not Classico) is possibly a fancy. There has been a suggestion that during the early Renaissance, wine was scented with iris petals, something that could well have been fashionable at the Medici court of the Grand Duke of Tuscany. That the modern Classico should have a hint of violets under the *consortium* rules suggests they are cognizant of historical sentiments, if not actually in concert with the principle. It's an opportunity for the purveyors of false hopes to use up a page or two of floral adjectives to describe them.

Whatever the case may be the practice of correcting the wine without such aromatic extravagances has taken many forms. Both Pliny and Cato advised the use of a boiled wine as a correction. The reason for this is not too clear as such a method reduces the alcohol from a liquid that has little sugar, unless it is a very sweet wine which leads us to a point we will take up later in respect of Roman wine in particular.

Vin Cotto is still made in some parts of Italy, notably Sicily in the South where it forms part of the process, required to make Marsala, though the practice seems unheard of in Tuscany.

Not quite in the sense of *Vin Cotto,* the boiling of wine does still take place - only more often as an expectorant for bronchial conditions. If you develop a chesty cough in Tuscany you may well be advised to undergo the initiation.

An inhalation of the sugar or honey-sweetened wine's steamy vapours with the soothing effect on your chest, and naturally the pleasant imbibing afterwards, is an old *podere* remedy that proves remarkably effective. Its existence might also help explain why apothecaries sold wine as a cordial in England during the Middle Ages. Ancient physicians are also known to have used wine as a medium for medicinal potions.

At this point, having surged ahead of the story again, we'll return to the final days of August where the cultivation at Sant'Anna is complete, and the vines left to rest in the sunshine with only the occasional palm of Benini to disturb them, testing the weight of a bunch while meditating upon the precious liquid contained within.

Our hasty excursion into the realms of the '*corretto*' will soon be slotted into place.

It's a time of much contemplation, and much discussion on what is fast approaching, that extraordinary Bacchanalian harvest festival, the *Vendemmia*.

54 litre demijohns.

When a Tuscan builder makes a nonsense of his work he most charmingly calls it *rustico*, meaning it's erratic in a rural sense, and thus in some way acceptable. All those tranquil and romantically converted farmhouses with a little peeling paint on the window frames, rickety shutters, terracotta tiles and gutters above wisteria covered stone walls, wouldn't present such an alluring, splendid and enchanting picture without their assistance. Tuscan builders are said to add age!

Pictures these days are more likely to be the more accessible photographs, of which millions must have been taken every year to record some passing event in the Tuscan countryside. Unfortunately, as very few photographs exist of a time in the declining years of the great *villa - fattoria* and its subject *poderi*, these poetic visual representations of rustic life have to be found in the works of painters, and in Italy, no image is more evocative than that of the harvest.

Clearly the subject has fascinated artists from time immemorial, and Italy led the revival in rural subjects during the Renaissance with artists like Giorgione and Bassano, but few have captured it quite so exquisitely as the later Italian school of painting known as the Macchiaioli: Ciardi, Signorini, Fattori, along with a string of other highly perceptive painters. That an art historian referred to them as related to the schools of Tachisme and Action Painting is remarkable and curious, for the end results could not be further removed from Jackson Pollock throwing buckets of paint at the canvas than a Pontormo is from a Picasso. It is, at the very least, a distorted view of the Macchiaioli's preliminary painting technique of initially smearing and blurring the colour of the undergrowth that will serve as background for a conventionally delineated subject.

One of the more successful of the Macchiaioli, Francesco Gioli, who spent a great deal of time in the countryside close to Volterra, produced works that perfectly express the valedictory romanticism of the period - *Autuno (1878); Vendemmia Volterra (1890);* and *Contadina tra le viti (1894),* to name a few. This last painting does not depict a vineyard so well tended as previously described, though the amorphous hedge of vines are definitely heavy with white grapes ready for the approaching harvest. As the pretty young girl appears to be on a bank above a steep ditch, this tends to underline a previous moot point on where the grapes were grown.

Needless to say, unlike the thoughts of some art historians, grapes are not just picked on a whim, or when the farmer feels inspired. They are particular about this sort of thing, and at Sant'Anna there is historically a tight window between the last week in September and the first week in October. Later, the risk of inclement weather increases exponentially. Waterlogged grapes do not make very good wine, even if they make a great deal!

For those interested in the comings and goings of the climate, until World War II the *vendemmia* in Tuscany was reckoned to begin on October 20th, a sure sign they had the benefit of longer summers. Benini can remember such periodic phases over the last half century, but considers scientific reasoning of little moment when beyond man's control. You just learn to live with change. As the harvests have been gathered earlier in the last few seasons, late September or early October, it may indicate a decade of some cooler weather. But no one will depend on it.

Benini will discuss with his family and friends the optimum moment for the harvest to take place. Like all decisions on the land they have a tendency to veer towards the critical. If the ripening process could be extended until the first week in October, leaving the grapes to peak in a still hot early autumn sun, an additional one percent of alcohol might be added to the wine. That is critical. But then, if it should chance to rain...!

Over the past half century, the red and white grapes have gradually found themselves grown promiscuously - meaning together, and side-by-side. Nothing, in such a matter, could be less professional than a small *podere*, yet the only disadvantage seems to be that it necessitates them all being picked at the same time, as those willing hands have other places, and other duties to attend to.

This normally requires a troublesome balance to be achieved for the exact moment of the *vendemmia*. Not surprisingly, the tasting of the grapes on which the decision is finally settled remains fairly crucial.

By mid-September, though the bunches of grapes have looked perfect to the eye for some time, with the beautiful deep purple bloom of the red, and the golden transparency of the white, they may not be perfect to Benini who breaks each of the sample grapes open, and smells the flesh before popping it into his mouth. There, he makes a veritable meal of the solitary grape, perhaps a little for show - he has an audience after all - but mostly for a good reason. His oscillating rosy cheeks are confirming what his nose has already decided. Where taste is eighty-percent smell, the grape in his mouth is merely agreeing with his initial judgment. On a small *podere* where nearly everything is by trial and error, such practices have been honed over the years into an instinctive skill. Not something that can be passed on to another generation, being learnt only from personal experience allied to the passage of time. Consider the matter of taste. How can you describe such a thing in reference to a grape, except in the most specious and superficial of terms?

From this it's fairly obvious that much depends on opportunity, and for the approaching harvest - given the pessimistic forecasts for autumn, and his own inclination - Benini opts for late September, while the weather seems fair.

The day, like the decision, comes in a rush. Having left the moment for as long as possible under a torrid sun, and deep blue sky, the appearance of an innocent cloud, albeit not quite as white as snow, stampedes everyone into a fit of activity.

On the farm the main priority is cleanliness, encompassing all requisites from the vats to the vine. The *cantina* is hosed down, and scrubbed, then hosed down again. It is not a time to be anywhere near the building - unless you have a free shower in mind. In the vineyard the tractor reappears with its bowser and spray attachments to wash the remains of any previous copper treatment from the clusters of grapes. This has been greatly assisted by stripping back the overhanging leaves prior to the harvest. Benini's obsession with keeping the superfluous foliage under control had demonstrated considerable foresight. He'd dismissed any groans at the thought of more pruning. In another life he probably went under the name of Figaro, that veritable Barber of Seville.

The work of the harvest is divided roughly into three parts. It can hardly be arbitrary, because there is no union demarcation on a small *podere*. People are there because they wish to be - with family, with friends, and with a great deal of good old-fashioned Italian *cameratismo*, or camaraderie.

Firstly there is the *Padrone*, the person in charge, known by his prominent figure, but not least, because he naturally organizes everyone. This appears to be a haphazard arrangement, which it is, after a fashion, but ultimately the decision will always be his. Benini confides that he has to be careful that any arrangements aren't quietly forgotten on the way. Too often he'll be led a good - natured dance by the volunteers who will have their own way of doing things. If the English are masters of the two-step, Italians are definitely masters of the side step.

In this respect it is almost like an orchestra, where Benini is the conductor, and all these sundry people are the musicians. Everyone is aware of their own task, and how it is expected to fit into place with all the various elements. Improvisation seems to be the most prominent.

All this translates into a liberty to work at one's own pace, giving a willing hand wherever needed, or to wherever the conversation happily takes you. Our *maestro* oversees this activity, only intervening - mostly with his own labour - when the oboes get too far ahead of the clarinets. Other than that, he is not an inconspicuous figure carrying the heavy crates for the ladies!

Secondly, the *cantina* manager - a temporary status conferred on the factotum, Nilo Bacci, - finds himself in charge of the extraction process with another factotum 'moonlighting' from another small farm. This will provide constant excitement, and Chaplinesque confusion, as they rush up and down ladders among the spaghetti like pipes and tubes feeding the juice into the selected vat. Both will be determined not to spill a drop, despite noisily arguing all the while.

They will also be particularly keen not to see any diversion from the steady flow of grapes, so when the momentum does occasionally slacken, it results in a protesting windmill of arms. An efficient delivery system for the fruit, something in the manner of a production line, guarantees their continuous arrival, and the reciprocal return of empty crates to be filled.

It is; therefore, essential that the third group, the pickers, should not be kept waiting for an empty crate when the ease of all manual labour is dependent on establishing a rhythm. Benini is certainly not very keen at this moment on any syncopated music in his orchestra.

Vendemmia - Grape picking.

The men generally work alone, heads down, while the women prefer to work in pairs, one on each side of the vine talking non-stop. They are often wonderfully large ladies built, as one wag put it, for comfort not speed. At least one part of this statement is untrue! Despite regular pruning the air is still filled with their good-humoured banter: much repetition of *"troppe foglie"* - 'too many leaves' as they neatly snip the culprits away to reach any hidden trusses of grapes. The resolute men are probably best on their own. The power of a pair of secateurs close to someone else's fingers doesn't bear thinking about. They also prefer to work with the sun behind them, on the lower, sloping part of the vineyard, which out of necessity is a solitary occupation. This way they can work through the vines to reach the lower bunches of grapes, saving the strain on their backs. An important matter when the carrying of grape laden crates puts a further strain on the spine. Staggering across the broken ground doesn't help, but the trick is not to let the weight dangle somewhere near the bottom of the stomach, but to hold it as high as possible above the centre of gravity.

The efficient ladies, meanwhile, carry the crate calmly between them.

The introduction of plastic crates has eliminated the

once timeless scene of woven wicker baskets almost half the size of their owners. You can still admire them, but only in the Macchiaioli paintings where the country *contadine* are slender *madonne* with a sense of colour long since lost to the modern world. Somehow, one has to admit, neither they, nor their towering *cesto di vimini,* would look quite so romantic beside a Fiat tractor.

Plastic crates.

The down side of the plastic crate is that they are not so easily disposed of when reaching the end of a useful life. Nor will plastic provide nutrition for the soil by being burnt, tending to end up as unsightly rubbish in the countryside, half covered in weeds, dumped behind a barn. One of the banes of modern life seems to be that so many materials and appliances are not reusable. Given the recycling, if not aesthetic genius of the Tuscan farmer, perhaps that is just as well.

Meanwhile the steady bark of the tractor's exhaust arriving at the head of the rows of vines, is followed by heavily punctuated silences while hands calmly unload its cargo of empty crates, replacing them with those that are full. The tractor's rhythmic rattling and wheezing away again in complete sonority, provides the perfect adagio to this unhurried tempo.

Elsewhere, the vast acres of commercial vineyards will have had recourse to temporary paid hands, being not yet as fully mechanized as Australia, where nearly all the grapes (and perhaps not a few lizards) are harvested by machinery. No doubt something is lost of the convivial fellowship that appears more entertainment than industry on a small *podere* still holding fast to their old traditions of family and friends.

Yet the labour of twelve months is a serious business for estate and *podere* alike. As both take it very seriously indeed, nature tends to look kindly on those who have taken the trouble to cosset and appreciate the potential in her moods. Neither is likely to squander this largesse by indifference.

Larger, professional vineyards, are; however, locked into a quite different philosophy. Price competition in their economy is intense, and maintaining an ancient economic model of production a restraint on maximizing profits. The cost of overproduction would have to be born somewhere, and given the vigorous marketing of their competitors, as such, can't all be passed on to the customer. This may not be apparent in Britain, but in Italy, supermarket shelves often groan under the weight of a wine that hardly costs more than the bottle it is in.

Yet, somehow, there appears to be room for them all. Many farmers realize that profits are more likely to come from producing a superb wine with kudos attached. Not 'off the peg', but 'bespoke', coming from small, select production. Such exclusivity can hardly be cheap. But it's not the only story. It's a different one. Estate wine is a cultural function, dependent as much on fashion as custom. On the other hand, 'superfluous' has to be paid for somewhere, and it's likely hiding under a familiar, inexpensive, but unreliable, trademark. The reason perhaps, for a considerable number of Italians to buy their everyday wine loose, without a label, and possibly why there are no statistics for *sfuso* consumption.

On the average *podere* harbouring a peasant tradition,

whether they come from one or not, there's a tendency to maximize the crop in much the same way as gardeners grow tomatoes, having in mind that enough is never enough. There will always be welcome hands to receive the surplus. Because there is no interest in ageing the product, exclusivity doesn't have to be expensive, so any excessive surplus of wine is very inexpensive indeed.

Despite this, Benini will have instructed the total dilettante on how to gather the grapes; not all perfect bunches dangling conveniently for the secateurs. He can't bear the thought of losing any. If this is the novice's first *vendemmia*, then they must keep a wary eye on their feet.

Given the concentration of their growth, the bunches of grapes have a habit of wrapping themselves with dogged determination tightly to the wire, or each other, by way of their strong curly tendrils - *viticci* - attached to the stalk, making them difficult to see among the remaining foliage. Severing such bunches takes practice, plus a little perseverance if one is to avoid ending up with a scattering of precious grapes by their boots, and the ire of 'our maestro'!

"Patience," he will say, "is a virtue you can afford." Not being hampered by piecework, there's really no argument. Even a few crates, bursting at the brim at the end of the day, will be considered a welcome contribution.

Diraspatrice.

As the grapes arrive at the cantina they are tipped into

the *pigiadiraspatrice*, or *diraspatrice* for short! Not surprisingly, there appears no equivalent English word. The term comes from the Italian *diraspare*, which quite literally means 'to pick grapes from the bunch', something many will have been doing to satisfy the little pangs of hunger that arrive about eleven o'clock after an eight o'clock start, and only a hurried coffee.

Perhaps the appliance is best described as a very large, horizontal mincing machine, that effectively strips the grapes from the stalks - *raspi* - and churns the fruit into a pulpy liquid, or 'must' described in the previous chapter. This pulpy, glutinous fluid, too dense and cloudy to be called wine, is pumped directly into the waiting vats.

So. Not a naked foot in sight.

Well, perhaps. The Romans apparently were not believed to tread their grapes, nor instructed their slaves in this manner, a practice that only seems to have been resorted to in poorer times. The collapse of the empire had a traumatic effect on the standard of civilization, not least on agriculture. Most of that regression has only been made up and improved in the last century, but there are a few rustic diehards even today, who persevere in the old ways - their perambulations, it is reported, can produce very drinkable results.

A fine fresco by the quattrocento Renaissance artist, Benozzo Gozzoli, in Pisa's Camposanto cemetery, has a detail demonstrating how the peasants trampled the grapes in that period. Even so, the young maiden delivering the fruit, though bare footed, doesn't appear impoverished by any means. Perhaps our concept of what signifies 'poor' has been distorted by time, and the progress of technology, which for the most part, is not much more than a hundred years old.

There is evidence that some of the ancients were not enamoured of footwork either, and arranged the quite simple method of using sheets as a tourniquet so they could wring the juice out of the grapes. Ancient inscriptions depict quite elaborate frameworks set up to maximize the compression provided by these machines. Nevertheless, the Egyptians, ever heavy on the footwork given the number of slaves with 'idle feet', seem to have also favoured 'treading troughs' illustrated in contemporary figurative scenes.

However this may be, ahead of their time the Romans

used a *torculum*, or press, of which a very fine example has been discovered at Pompeii, so both methods - foot, and mechanical, press - have been used in Italy at some period. Modern equivalents called *torchio*, also made of wood, were still being used in the second half of the twentieth century. From there the juice was strained into a large vat to ferment called a *lacus*, (Latin for lake, so perhaps open). Made of wood or pottery, they demonstrate the speed of the revolution that has taken place in the vineyard. Little improvement seemed to have been made in their construction by the time of the Renaissance.

Torchio. Ancient wooden grape press.

As the morning lengthens into noon at Sant'Anna, the faint murmur of *"pasto di mezzogiorno"*, a soft but plaintive cry for lunch, becomes a disembodied, if far from disgruntled mutter through the vineyard. It is also apparent that some of the ladies have been missing for some time past, an example of the infallible discretion of Italian women, appreciating and undertaking what needs to be done. In rural Italy, food still takes an important social position in the working day; accomplished with the least possible disturbance to their way of life.

Being a small vineyard, Sant'Anna is normally capable

of being cleared before dusk, which is in itself a small problem. Not many Italians like to tackle a very large meal at eight o'clock in the evening, especially in Tuscany, where the traditional main meal, or *pranzo,* is taken at lunchtime.

This was not always so. In the Roman world, *pranzo* from *prandium* indicated a late breakfast - a little like our 'brunch', not the modern Italian lunch. *Cena,* now best described as supper, was the principal meal of the Romans and originally taken at noon, but in the following indulgent and intemperate times of the empire, consumed from the late afternoon. Starting at five o'clock, and sometimes four, it lasted well into the evening. Today, northern Europeans being invited for *cena* in the evening are surprised, having taken a light lunch in expectation of a dinner at eight o'clock, to be indulged with a light supper!

Though changing life styles, and northern European eating habits, have seriously effected the regions from Piedmont to the Trentino, especially the hyperactive Milan, central and southern regions seem determined to hold steadfastly to their old traditions for a little while longer, at least.

Gluttony is not a particular Italian habit, but if it is a *festa* like the *vendemmia,* or they have guests, the meal, even when simple and rustic, will be gargantuan.

In fact, if 'simple' and 'rustic' are what sybaritic foreigners, satiated with experimental Grande Cuisine delight in, then the *vendemmia* is the right place to experience the opposite extreme. However, as hard work is a prerequisite, and deserving of a healthy appetite, they will probably balk at the opportunity, for unlike Shakespeare's Orlando 'chewing the food of sweet and bitter fancy', it may prove a diversion not quite 'as you like it'!

XII: Pranzo

This might be described as a very loud chapter. Among rural Italians, the *vendemmia* meal is a noisy, tumultuous affair, and that held at Sant'Anna in a large wine vault or *cantina* is no different. With its shallow, barrel vaulted ceiling, and terracotta floor providing the perfect echo chamber, the hubbub defies conversation in any meaningful sense. A lip reading facility is; therefore, essential.

At the command *'A TAVOLA',* 'to the table', a maelstrom of bodies are caught up in a mad rush, being thrust at precipitate speed through the door, and into the room like swirling dervishes, until everyone manages to find themselves seated round a long wooden table in the traditional country fashion, and also in Italy the ancient social custom, where men and women sit separated from each other at the same table. One gathers swiftly that it more likely represents a sensible feminine rejection of sitting among a herd of hungry buffaloes, where food becomes a slapstick affair, rather than any nod towards tradition. One or two of the lighter souls, have to be patiently inserted somewhere before all are ready.

As the culinary odours had penetrated the short distance from the kitchen to the vineyard, all the appetites had been mysteriously stimulated and teased by those invisible aromatic vapours. Though the odour of ingredients at some point, might have been far from appetizing.

As an example, garlic happens to be the reverse of Indian 'Bombay Duck', though it is idle to contrast the alarming odour of Bengal's famous salted fish, something like the interior of an old wellington, with the lack of any such smell in garlic clothed in the shell of its natural state, evil or otherwise. Neither has the bald potato anything to recommend it, until the application of some heat.

It is more than an idle suggestion that cooking is akin to the making of wine - improving the material as a stimulant to the major senses. In the hands of a competent cook, all these examples are transformed into an agonizingly tempting aroma, designed to invigorate gastric juices from wherever they normally abide. Its influence on the food is a foregone conclusion.

From this you can gather that the Latin expression, *'sauvitatem cibi sentire',* which advises you to 'feel the flavour of food', is not as strange as it sounds.

The table has been covered by a large linen tablecloth, the centre copiously scattered within the reach of an arms length by the distribution of a variety of miscellaneous sized bottles of wine, some of a weighty 2 litres, others in the form of lighter straw covered *fiaschi.* They are predominantly red, despite the vineyard offerings being predominantly white. The ubiquitous plastic bottles of water are just as numerous, and it is apparent that country Tuscans generally opt for natural water, rather than the effervescent. The distinctive, and very Tuscan 'Uliveto', sourced from the *terme* on the old road from Cascina to Pisa, though highly popular, is a little too expensive to be found at an agricultural revel.

The important thing confirmed with the first course - *antipasti* - is that you are expected to help yourself. If anyone appears a little too modest, they will find their plate heaped up from all directions in an effort to kick - start their appetite. Neither is the wine an inanimate object; it is there to be moved, and as such, holds true at both ends of the table. Apart from that, everyone is left to his, or her, own devices.

Elizabeth David, no less an authority, insisted that Italian *antipasti* contained some of the most successful achievements in European cooking. Without a doubt, it is the glory of Italian cuisine. Infinitely resourceful in ingredients, they can turn the mundane into a rich and extravagant relish. The English, to their credit, are as equally enamoured of the simple, and the Italians have taken simplicity to the absolute extreme. Surely, a single sage leaf battered and fried, must be a lesson in epicurean modesty.

Yet perfection is not always preference, and many find a simple *affettati misti* - slices of cured meats in the form of prosciutto and salamis that have been long out of the refrigerator to regain their flavour, - set on the table in giant oval dishes, the ideal place to start.

If you consider the following description confusing, remember that the meal is very often prepared by many diverse souls all adding their portion to the feast. The *vendemmia* is often, in such a sense, a community event of great variety.

To hand are thick slices of chunky *Fiorentina* salami;

Tuscan *finocchiona,* a coarse salami heavy with wild fennel; hand made *sbriciolona* that cannot be sliced too thinly in case it falls apart; chocolate brown *Biroldo,* a Lucchese pigs blood speciality made from the head, and 'odds-and-bobs'; *soppressata* (see appendix), even if not classified as a true salami, being made from various boiled pieces of pork and beef, salted and pressed like brawn so that it resembles crazy paving is; nevertheless, included so that they all overlap in splendid disarray.

Other dishes will hold mouth watering lard laden slices of cured hams fresh from the bone, salty and still with their rinds of pepper and faint hum of garlic, surrounded by little *salsicce di cinghiale,* - sausages of wild boar covered in tough, dark brown skin, that stripped away reveals the makings of a gastronome's paradise.

If all this sounds extravagant, one look at the local supermarket *gastronomia,* with its confusing array and variety of *salume* (cold cuts of pork), should persuade you otherwise. Half a dozen different examples of an *etto* (100 grams) here, and an *etto* there, will not break the bank, and represents an excellent and simple way to commence a supper party if you're lost for inspiration.

There will be bowls of sliced Ogen melons, and for the sweeter tooth, a few figs. These will be late remainders from the vineyard, planted to suppress hunger when the next meal was still distant, and so ripe that their skins are studded with tiny granules of sugar, and burst asunder. Almost too delicate to pick up they are readily wrapped with *prosciutto* to make them manageable, so negating the modern Tuscan prejudice that only sybaritic northern Europeans mix meat with fruit.

Add to this a never ending supply of salt-less *pane casalingo,* bread not actually made in the home, but excellent from the local baker - identified by its scruffily authentic carbon marks, the result of being baked in a wood oven - and the cardiologist's warnings look dire indeed. Stray slabs of the extraordinary Ligurian bread, *'Focaccia',* glistening with salt and dripping with olive oil have somehow been smuggled in, and as soon, vanished.

The barrage of noise surges to an even greater fortissimo, just as an extra slice of *prosciutto* is contemplated, for the steaming *Pici* has arrived with its almost obligatory *ragù,* (not to be confused with ragoût - which uses pieces of meat to make a stew) a highly seasoned minced meat sauce, that for some esoteric culinary reason, cannot be replicated anywhere else.

The knowledgeable Benini explains that the trick lies in double mincing the meat. It is quite satisfactory purchasing regular mincemeat from the butcher; you just have to give it another turn. The highly flavoured taste, he adds, is sometimes down to the finely chopped chicken livers combined with a good handful of parsley. He is a rare soul in Tuscany. Not unheard of, but still rare - the practical domestic male cook. Knowledgeable there are plenty - every masculine arbiter knows about this culinary magic, being an expert in the transient genius of his mother. Unhappily, such genius rarely resides in the son.

The heavy, double folded, cord like pasta made with durum wheat used in this dish is reputed to be an invention of the Etruscans, and the original pasta. The material itself proclaims a long ancestry. The Etruscan connection with Egypt - emphasized in their early art and architectural details before they assimilated the Greek influence - suggests an original source of hard wheat made possible by the annual inundation of the Nile Valley. Whether it was an early hybridization from domesticated Emmer wheat would be difficult to say, but it is likely the closest relation to the original. The Emmer wheat grown today in the Garfagnana above Lucca is known as Farro. A unique characteristic of durum wheat is its yellow endosperm that gives it a pale honey colour.

If something more positive in the way of proof is required of its ancient provenance then you must visit the Ninth Century B.C. Cerveteri, lying within the province of Rome, where it is almost a coastal town with ports at Santa Severa and Palo. Amongst the many mausoleums, you will find the tomb of the Matuna family sculpted out of the stone tufa, including such items as couches, cushions, even slippers on the floor - all carved in situ. In one of its hollowed out 32 rooms, will be found walls and pillars covered in three-dimensional painted stucco reliefs depicting domestic Etruscan life. These include a table (Medieval: *spiantora*) used to make the pasta dough, with knives, rolling pin, and a crenulated pasta wheel, similar to those used by pasta cooks today to make *regnette* or *pappardelle.*

Some American cookery book writers have the unfortunate habit of referring to pasta as noodles, which they most certainly are not. The Chinese are not thought to have been familiar with durum wheat, as it is positively absent in noodles, which traditionally use plain (white) flour or rice flour. Historically, in China, noodles also appear to have been made from millet.

Commercially produced, *pici* is not everywhere available. Having an unusual character with the texture of *gnocchi* when cooked, the strands require more than a twirl of the fork. As they are exceedingly long and heavy, this is something of an adventure.

Hardly having mastered this technical operation, the chefs arrive with what is perceived to be the deceptively named *Fagioli con salsicce.* Two large ladle scoops of white haricot beans are turned steeply onto the plate - that is all! Where are the sausages?

As the experienced members of the group seem to be preparing for something more, it is obviously best not to be caught out. Replenishing the glass with wine, and arming oneself with the thickest chunk of bread available, appears to fully equip you for the next bout - which is just as well.

The sausages, straight from the wood-burning oven, make a precarious entrance, being wheeled round the table amid much cheering. Huge alpine mounds of rich, charred, piping hot, Tuscan hand made pork filled 'bangers', cut from metre long strings that, if good behaviour selects one will have two more added to the plate by the cook. Three is the absolute minimum! (There are a number of recipes for this particular dish. If the sausages have been added to the beans to cook they will be unctuously softer in texture. They are excellent, nevertheless.)

At this juncture the cooks will appreciate that the gastric juices have done enough rounds and need to avoid a knock out. While it is true that the wine, some retrieved from forgotten recesses bottled two years ago, and still with a not unpleasant bite, have managed to pacify the gastronomic indulgences between bouts, we have to agree something more curative would not go amiss.

Enter the splendidly green and red - *Insalatina di Campo,* - a salad of curly *indivia* or endive, a ragged lettuce called *scarola,* and wild *rucola,* or rocket, arbitrarily mingling with chopped *radicchio rosso,* a type of chicory. Thereafter, it was blessed with a sprinkling of a traditionally simple Tuscan dressing, - the *podere* oil mixed with wine vinegar. It is worth saying that this form of dressing, shaken and not stirred, is merely for convenience sake during a large gathering. Classically, the vinegar comes first and is mixed well into the salad before adding the oil. Not a few cooks believe that, in this manner, it neutralizes any bacteria that may have escaped the necessary rinsing. Be that as it may, the dressing instantly produced a much more settling effect on the thoroughly abused stomachs.

After this necessary chastening, everything slows to a decent pedestrian pace. The choice between a heavenly light, vanilla dusted, sponge *Torta*, or a massively flavour laden blackberry jam lattice work *Crostata*, is difficult. Any lack of due diligence, means both! There is Grappa or Vin Santo with the ubiquitous *Cantuccini*, a hard, sweet biscuit laden with almonds, a local version of the traditional *Biscotti di Prato*, and thick black Mocca coffee to put it all to rights - before someone rudely mentions that there are still some grapes that need picking.

The return to the vines will be a desultory affair, and after two more hours with half a dozen rows of vines remaining, Benini must call it a day. No matter, tomorrow morning will see the work finished by a stalwart few, along with the still ample remains of today's feast.

Benini and Nilo Bacci wandered back to the cantina looking very content with themselves having brought another splendid 'harvest home'. But they still have one important responsibility to oversee before they can 'call it a day'.

The initial stage in the making of wine has not varied a great deal from that of old, except that the equivalent vats are both sealed allowing the fermentation to take place under pressure. When the vats for the initial stage of the *vendemmia* are full, they are capped with a pressure valve or *bollitore*. This is a water seal, originally in glass, now in a translucent polyethylene plastic, that acts as a one-way valve. The sound of the escaping gas makes a popping noise, rather like porridge coming to the boil - *bollire*. Remembering that the concrete vats are nearly forty years old, any leaks that develop round the seal have to be contained using flexible mastic. As such a method is not foolproof; thereafter, it will need a regular inspection.

But for the moment they are able to place the caps on the vats and tighten down the *bollitore.* Quite naturally there is a small argument over how much water to add in creating the one-way seal, before all is happily resolved, and the vats are left to quietly slumber.

It will not be for long.

Bollitore.

Thankfully, at last, there is time for a tired soul to slip away to a quiet corner, stretch out on the side of the hill, back to the warm earth, stomach still so full you're embarrassed not to see your toes, and breathe a contented sigh. The faint yeasty scent of crushed grapes hangs heavily in the air among the empty vines, while the lurid red sunset has cast the horizon into soft black outlines.

There is an unfamiliar and extraordinary feeling of reaching back; of being encompassed by a shift in time; a mental evocation suspending the physical world you normally reside in, yet contiguous with a tradition that has been a domestic feature of this region for over three thousand years. It seems as durable as the stones that have raised its cities, and shrugged off the passage of three civilizations.

But you cannot ignore the evidence that these are now only vestiges of a transient way of life; fragments scattered in Tuscany's odd corners, too fragile to long exist in a changing technological world.

Such thoughts are accompanied by a rising melancholy, for in this changing fashion not many Tuscans are quite so romantic about returning to the soil, only about a Utopian ideal that lingers in some hidden part of their imagination.

But just for the moment you can appreciate what it's like to share that ancient hope for the harvest, if not an image of their private dreams.

The hills in the foreground are gradually becoming misty purple folds, smudged green and umber, rippling with the grey striations of Tuscan *calanchi*. Behind, dark and dense with ancient bosco, the perspective becomes a voluptuous brooding spirit watched over by that mysterious aerial fortress you'll find described in Macaulay's 'Lays':

> From lordly Volterrae
> Where scowls the far-famed hold
> Piled by the hands of giants
> For godlike kings of old.

XIII: In the Lap of the Gods

With the passing of the *vendemmia* there begins a critical time in the processing of the grapes. Recalling that Sant'Anna has 0.5 hectare (1.25 acres) under vines, the year's *vendemmia* produced fifty *quintali* of grapes, (a *quintale* is a shade under 2 hundred weight), which represents one hundred *quintali* per hectare.

Commercial producers are often inclined to halve this yield as their economic interests are focused on improving the quality of their wine - fewer grapes patently translates into a greater percentage of the sustenance provided by the vine reaching selected fruit. That is one aspect of a value added formula, a step beyond the experience of our journey.

Creativity is not the sole calling of the artist, and though many parts of the experience have been critical in determining the outcome, few are filled with such tense excitement as this: the changing of grape juice into that wonderful red or white liquid - wine!

The number of things that can go wrong are legion, and they might happen today, or tomorrow, or any time in the next three or four months. Luckily, only the first ten to fifteen days of the first fermentation are critical. After that, the wine's fate is subject to the slow process of vigilant care and attention.

At this point, the story reveals a complicated technical journey. Having previously relied on agronomy, and the good nature of the elements, it now passes into a period solely dependent on the skill or artistry of the wine maker, and the creation of those particular nuances they ultimately hope to achieve. Some will approach it with scientific precision, others with the calm contemplation of experience. Whatever skills they bring to the task in hand will ultimately determine whether the results meet with your approval or not.

This, then, is where Sant'Anna finds itself. Benini had made sure that the grape juice, or pre fermentation 'must', had been safely transferred to the vats, all the caps had been screwed down, and the *bollitore*, or pressure valve, made secure. Then fingers were crossed.

The *cantina* seemed awfully quiet.

Fermentation is created by micro-organisms, or yeast, held in the bloom on the skin of the grape whose excreted enzymes consume the natural sugar, resulting in the creation of heat which produces the chemical change into ethanol (alcohol).

This misty grey veil of bloom is more noticeable on the red grape, though it is as prevalent on the white. Its purpose besides preventing the loss of moisture is as a repository for the yeast. Small country vineyards prefer this natural form or 'ambient yeast', while commercial vineyards may well use cultured yeasts in an effort to provide more predictable results.

The colour pigment is held in the skin, and not in the grapes flesh. Unless a rosé is desired, where generally white and red grapes are blended, the simple choice of grape will determine the colour of the wine in the glass.

Having said that, this doesn't always seem to be the case where white wine is concerned. Passing along the rows of shelves in a wine shop refuses to produce many examples, if any, of that which resembles the true colour of nearly all white grapes.

Now, the observant will notice that 'white' *sfuso* has generally a very distinctive yellow tint; whereas, commercially produced dry white wine may have only a mere hint of the marigold about it. Indeed some, besides the difference in taste, may well have the appearance of water!

The answer lies, once more, in the skin. The colour of white wine can be controlled by removing the skin, or by the careful choice of light skinned grapes. That is why if you process skinless red grapes you'll produce 'white' wine.

Having removed the skin there will obviously be a short fall in micro-organisms, and to correct this problem it is necessary to add cultured yeast.

As this has nothing to do with *sfuso*, being a trick too far, we won't pursue it.

Where this aversion to the natural colour of white wine came from, bar the obvious, has not been elicited, but it's never been of any concern to the Tuscan farmer, whose vines providing the thirst quenching amber nectar, remains one of the delightful pleasures of summer.

The fermentation, which normally takes place in two stages, generates an ever-perennial problem of vast quantities of a dangerous gas, Carbon Dioxide - CO2.

Strangely enough, being part of the Oxygen Cycle, we

couldn't live without it!

Despite this, and besides being a common food additive that finds its way into nearly all carbonated soft drinks for example, carbon dioxide in the form of dry ice manages to reappear in the vineyard where, if crushing is not going to be immediate, it can be used to cool down the grapes to prevent the spontaneous fermentation that would otherwise take place.

Benini relates the story of Florio, one of the farm dogs who had the misfortune of being inadvertently locked inside the cantina until found the next morning, prostrate, and nearly dead. You can breathe it out, but you cannot breathe it in. We have to leave the tricky business of converting such deadly gases in the good hands of the sun and chlorophyll molecules abounding in trees and plants whose photosynthetic action helps oxidize water into oxygen.

This salutary lesson at least ensures that the *cantina* has its foul air religiously removed before anyone deigns to enter. Though in itself a careful exercise, and cognisant that changes in temperature can have a marked effect on the fermentation, the reality is that practical considerations do not allow for a small *podere* to achieve the clinical control of temperature practiced by professional vineyards who must squeeze the last litre of wine and income from the *vendemmia*. 'Profit and loss accounts are the stuff of competent management, but the item referred to as closing stock - unsold items - is a 'hang over' they can do without.

Nevertheless, grand *azienda* or small *podere*, as the fermentation begins to heat things up some effort must be made to ensure it doesn't get out of hand.

Yeast growth ceases in red wine at approximately 29.4°C, and in white at a much lower 15.3°C. Kept some degrees below these the liquid clears more quickly, produces alcohol, and suffers less from bacterial infection. So it pays to mitigate the worst effects of heat by a little draught.

That; however, is not quite so simple as it sounds. This is a matter of some precision. Too fast a drop in temperature has the same result as raising it - a serious effect on fermentation. Everything on a *podere* is a balancing act, and subject to that ancient law - experience. Thermostats and heat extraction being in the realm of wizardry, it can't be anything too technical. Just knowing which way the wind is blowing, and which window to leave open, and by how much!

At the point of initial fermentation patience has to be added to the expectation; for like a steam engine waiting until the system is sufficiently pressurized by boiling water, so does the vat - except in this case such work is carried out by the frantic little enzymes beavering away within. Everyone is waiting for the first tiny detonation in the *bollitore*. This may take some hours, even into the next day, and anxious faces will come and go, enquiring if the fermentation has started. They all know it must happen - if there's going to be a vintage!

The fermentation process is not a constant, and the ambient temperature will speed up or retard its progress. To a great degree the material used for the vat also affects this. For example, fermentation will be quicker in stainless steel vats, with their thinner walls, than those of concrete. To achieve some consistency, and balance, it is more efficient to use one type or the other during this period.

The initial fermentation takes perhaps eight to ten days for red grapes, and considerably more for white, as long as fifteen days.

During this period Benini becomes even more attentive. A constant visitor to the *cantina*; drawing off a small quantity of liquid to inspect; holding the glass against the light; tasting, but not drinking the contents. Understandably, given the agitated changes that are taking place. Nevertheless, he must put any pained expression behind him; getting it right the first time. If the fermentation stops too early it can be restarted, but the wine will almost certainly be inferior in quality. He likens the event to a tenor breaking on a high 'C'. The show will go on, but represents something of a tragedy.

In a very poor season, which luckily does not happen so often, a product known as *Metabisofito* could be added. The action subdues the vinegar (*aceto*) enzyme and invigorates the sugar enzymes, thus raising the level of the alcohol. This is not something to contemplate with any affection.

As temperatures during these stages are critical, it's always possible, given fluctuations in the weather, that the process will be interrupted before an acceptable level of alcohol has been reached. If the wine carries a faint odour of the brewery, or has a cloying sweetness, then it has been stopped too early, and must be reactivated.

When the bubbling finally stops in the *bollitore*, so has the first fermentation. Then it really is all "hands to the pump", and the *vino fiore* - the wine from this initial fermentation - drawn rapidly off and transferred to empty vats. Essentially, this is done at once to avoid the vinegar bacteria *Acetobacter*, (from *Acetum*, the Latin for vinegar) feeding on the dead yeast and turning the 'must' into acetic acid.

A little of this *Madre del Vino* - Mother of the wine - finds its way into the Italian country kitchen to be added to superfluous wine; swiftly turning the liquid into vinegar. You can still purchase attractive terracotta jugs with a vitreous glazed liner for this purpose, but they are not to be altogether trusted. The vinegar can too readily eat through a thin slip messily leaching its contents to the outside.

At this stage the drawn liquid is cloudy, but at least free from the 'must'. The still considerable amount of fine debris held in suspension will take some time to sink to the bottom of the new vat during the secondary fermentation. Only then will the liquid have the appearance of a bottled wine.

Not many nowadays will go along with the old folklore: 'Better muddy wine than clear water.'

Vinaccia.

Left at the bottom of the previous vat after the initial fermentation are the remnants of skin and pulp, a combination of waste that is sometimes referred to as *vinaccia.* The latter must not be confused with Vernaccia, a white grape from San Gimignano; itself not to be confused with Vernaccia from just about everywhere else!

Strettoio.

There will be approximately 100 litres trapped inside this multi coloured cake that is not going to be lost after all the hard work in producing it. Removed from the vat it is packed into an open wooden staved press, the *strettoio,* which is screwed down by hand, or hydraulically driven, by a press.

The liquid obtained by this squeezing is called *vino stretto,* after the device. The only difference between *stretto* and *fiore* is that the pressed wine, coming from the skin, will be of a darker colour. Locally, they are treated in exactly the same way.

Buried in the 'must', the fermentation of the *stretto* has been delayed, necessitating that the small quantity extracted be transferred to demijohns of 54 litres capacity with their own mini *bollitore* pushed tightly over the neck for the fermentation to be completed.

A little more on these magnificent glass bottles: the early ones were hand made by glass blowers, and readily identified by their rather pear like shape, long 'snapped off' necks and molten glass necklaces that some say indicated the craftsman's signature. The name is said to be a corruption of the French 'Dame Jeanne'. These voluptuous *damigiane* are invisible in their wooden *vestiti*, or jackets, stuffed with straw, standing on a low platform of wood from where they can be siphoned off into other containers below. Very often they are also found standing forlornly next to a council dustbin. A sure sign that an old *podere* has been sold, or changed hands.

Because *sfuso* is a wine for the year and not intended for ageing, the fermentation process might be thought to be different from the wine that will be left to mature. This is not the case, and any manipulation of the process generally takes place after the second fermentation that is identical for both until a decision is made of either choosing to create the wine as *sfuso*, or place it in wood for ageing.

All wine has a vintage, but at Sant'Anna they are saved such pressing acknowledgements by not having much of an option - it's made to drink, and the sooner the better. Despite this, they can still be heard eulogizing over one exceptional year or another; generally when the percentage of alcohol has been such that it acquires an awesome, and generally dubious, reputation!

Until the fermentation is complete it takes place in concrete vats, or more recently, in stainless steel. As already mentioned the latter are especially desirable, not only for the reduction in labour, but because the control of unhealthy microorganisms is made easier. The advantage of sterile cleansing, leaving a spotless container with nothing to contaminate next year's wine, has greatly improved the quality of *sfuso*. In this modern 'green' age, they probably also save millions of litres of water throughout the region.

Like 'old soldiers'; however, the concrete vats seem not to die, but merely fade away. It's going to be some time before they are replaced completely, and perhaps only when the old way of life finally ceases.

Wooden casks were changed for the new concrete vats in most *podere* after the Second World War when the luxury of *cantina* staff was no longer omnipresent in the changing commercial and social climate. Large families might still be the norm, but they couldn't be sustained on the minute, newly independent *podere*. Some of these leviathan replacements demonstrate an unwillingness to genuflect to the new, being cast in the shape of a barrel complete with integral look-a-like riveted expansion hoops and raised chime. Others favoured a more architectural approach, square or oblong, with classically restrained fielded panels.

Examples in every age, and every trade, demonstrate a desire to hang on to the past for as long as it can. One can still marvel at those intricate cast iron 'Gothic' structures supporting stationary steam engines.

Such vats don't add anything to the wine, being completely neutral, but then, this loss of taste is also partly shared by wooden barrels after some years of use. However, wood still breathes, allowing the complex transfer of oxygen - in both directions. Too much evaporation can leave the wine exposed to the ingress of air, and in danger of becoming oxidized, the bane of small producers who welcomed the labour saving possibilities of concrete and stainless steel.

This has not been lost on commercial producers, who choose to use stainless steel tanks with short periods of barrel ageing if necessary, before bottling those wines not intended for serious improvement. For longer periods of ageing the level of the wine and volume of air at the head of the barrel (ullage) is controlled by topping up. A highly skilful chore that is not required from the maker of *sfuso*.

Though no longer an important component in the *podere cantina*, because of the historical relationship, some aspects of the wooden barrels association and function are of passing interest.

Large as some of these wooden containers are, none seem able to match the possible exaggeration noted by the Greek geographer, Strabo, who declared that in Gallia Cisalpina (Gaulish northern Italy) wine was so abundant that the wooden vessels in which it was commonly stored were the size of small houses! Well, that at least confirms wooden barrels were in use c. 64 B.C., even if Strabo managed to inflate their proportions by comparing them to a small bungalow!

Modern barrels can still be impressively large, making a large dent in the vineyard's budget. Hand made 1000 gallon sizes (4000 litres) may cost over £9000. At that price, things are getting very serious. The 15000 gallon behemoth one daren't ask about! (See appendix.)

Podere farmers seem reluctant to dispose of their wooden monuments - pushing them up into the corner of the cantina, black with noble age, gathering nothing but rust on the hoops, and multi-layers of dust everywhere else. There, they continue to remind you that once all wine was 'oaked', or occasionally 'castanated', in chestnut (*castagna*) barrels. No doubt such *sfuso* was a very different beast than consumed today.

When these wooden barrels were in use for many years the flavour of the wood soon diminished, though other chemical reactions continued to take place. This raised a problem, firstly of taste and secondly of expense, which gave rise to a certain amount of legerdemain.

There are those who insist that a good wine should 'taste of the wood', but in reality it should have a pronounced overlaying taste of fruit. Which fruit might be difficult to say, but you will know it's not acorns!

Apparently, no oenologist worth his salt would consider creating such a thing, relying as they do on the wood to bring out the essence of the grapes. If so, they would probably then agree that if the taste is heavily tainted with oak - an exaggerated intrusion - then there's probably something wrong with it. This, of course, refers to Italian wine, as some vineyards in Spain prefer long maturation in casks, and very pronounced 'woodiness'.

Indeed, oenologists very often seek to enhance the fruitiness of a wine to balance out the oak and tannin present, especially when barriqued in new small barrels.

But some oenologists do not, and when you consider that a large majority of wine drinkers might well have difficulty telling a Bordeaux from a Burgundy, let alone a Carmignano from a Chianti unless they could read it on the label, then some sophistry does not go amiss with the odd accountants who must balance the books.

Wood is the one thing we will soon have learnt to recognize in tasting a wine. Unhappily, it is a self - defeating experience if we rely too heavily on its presence. The fact that the great wines of the world are all aged, having spent some time in wood, rather obfuscates the stubborn reality that so have most of the worst.

We will know when a wine has been overindulged with wood. Strong tastes are insidious, and there is considerable difficulty telling the difference between one over-oaked wine from another. Oak can, quite simply, be used as a mask for a poor vintage by an unscrupulous vineyard.

In this it has sadly become the yardstick for too many of us who enjoy a glass of wine but don't have the wherewithal to expand our appreciation of wine nonpareil. It's a problem not easily solved. One can only hope that we don't solely drink wine just because it's wine; that is without consideration or appreciation, though on occasion, when time or pocket demands it, there may be some justification in that!

But hopefully, we will stop and think: what of that most important ingredient of all, the grape? Is it Barbera, or Sangiovese, or Nebbiolo, for example? They have very particular flavours, even as *sfuso*, and there you can 'learn your trade', so to speak.

A farm *sfuso* will not have been tampered with in a search for greater markets, and more often will reflect the fruit accurately. In such a process it should not have been lost through ageing, so it can give great satisfaction when you recognize them in a vintage wine. If you don't, it is just as interesting to discover the dominant grape, or even be apprised of a blend that has proved equally pleasing. Just as long as you're not content to merely note that if a wine tastes of oak, it must be good.

This affection for ageing, by inference, can be firmly laid at the door of St Luke - 'No man having drunk old wine straight away desireth new, for he sayeth, the old is better.' (Luke V.5).

This argument between youth and maturity leaves true wine lovers perplexed. They possibly would concur with H.W.Yoxall's musical analogy (which would please Benini despite his critical objection) that all wine strikes a note on the palate: good wine strikes a chord, fine wine plays a diatonic scale, while great wine plays a chromatic one. But then, he was talking about Burgundy. Poor wine, not being mentioned, one assumes was seriously out of tune!

St. Luke's contemporary, St Peter, who is said to have passed secretly through Tuscany, credibly spending a night or two in Volterra with the family of his successor, the then young and impressionable, Lino, might well have been informed of a quite different opinion if he consumed and discussed the local wine.

Tuscan farmers brought up on *sfuso* contradict that saintly pomposity with a local controversial proverb that Benini whispers discreetly in case the *signore* overhear:

I vini sono come le donne
Più giovane sono meglio sono,
Più che invecchiano
Peggio sono.

Wine is like women
The younger they are the better they are
The older they get
The worse they are.

This, in fact, may not be entirely a male prejudice, even if it is crudely insensitive. If the preferred wine is young, then its youth does in fact provide one of the interesting aspects of *sfuso*. One must only consider the obvious difference between an expected adolescent vigour, and the refined elegance of a wine that has spent some appropriate time in wood, to recognize the veritable parting of the ways. Some would say it is the end of science, and the beginning of the art of wine making.

Despite this, Benini smiles warmly at having his attention drawn to the old barrels, and relates the history of the *tino* standing vertically, wide at the base and tapering to an open top. Being used for the initial fermentation of the 'must', and because it was unable to create any pressure within, *buccia*, the skin or peel, rose to the top where it wasn't effective. Therefore, twice a day, and very often during the night, wielding a wooden impeller, or *frollatura*, the floating pulp had to be pushed down again to where it was needed.

This process continued for about ten days with a red wine, sometimes less, until the termination of the first fermentation, when it was ready for transferring to another vat as new wine - *Vino Fiore.*

Colloquially, the first fermentation was known as *tumultuoso* on account of the pyrotechnics going on inside the barrel, and *malolattica* when things had calmed down during the second fermentation.

There seems to have been an advantage with this open method, now lost by the use of modern vats, in that the problems caused by tannin was less likely. The fermentation, Benini explained, could be controlled by manipulating the quantity of skin or peel present in the grape juice by pushing the material back into the 'must' or, conversely, by skimming some off; therefore, in one way or the other, controlling the conversion into alcohol.

Its partner, lying horizontally, and known as a *botte* where the secondary fermentation took place, was sealed so the *vino fiore* could stand for about three months if red, five months if white. These figures represent a point where the wine is potable, not when they are at their peak, which is a quite different matter.

As a person has to eventually crawl inside the barrel, through what appears to be a very small aperture at the front to clean the interior, one imagines it was a role reserved for a small Dickensian child like Oliver Twist, but, hopefully, not under the care of someone like the vicious sweep Ganfield!

The Romans invariably marked each cask of wine with the name of the Consul, or the year made. Horace in his ode 'To a Cask' tells us that the wine it contained was from the Consulship of Manlius.

There were a number of consuls so named during this period. In this respect, the date would have been more helpful. As his friend, Corvinus, demanded his mellowest wine (in that period the older the better), he would have had the necessity to seek it in the furthest corner of his cellar, where it probably nestled with the traditional cup of Falernum wine, so beloved by Virgil.

That particular wine grown today close to the coast, just over the border of Latium into Campania on the old Via Appia, is not so exceptional, but we know nothing about the old to say if it was better. Indeed, no one is even sure if it is the same variety of grape.

If the illusive consul inscribed on Horace's cask was an L. Manlius Torquatus, 65 B.C., we can suppose that Horace's cask might have been laid down by his parents in the year of his birth. Oh for such parents now!

The *vino fiore* at that time was refined by mixing it with egg yolks, though the ratio, or quantity, does not seem to have been handed down to us. It is doubtful if a 'dozen standard' would suffice; nor can we express an opinion whether they were talking chicken or duck eggs! The albumen was not wasted either, being used to clear murky white wine.

Whatever it was, there seems to have been a quantum change in opinion, for as late as the nineteenth century, albumen was being used for the same refining purpose. The Dutch drink, Advocaat, is made from egg yolks and wine (also spirits) but the concoction, to look at, resembles more egg than anything else. The precursor must surely have been the infamous eggnog, made with Brandy and Rum amongst other things, and whisked into any hot beverage.

As the Romans invariably mixed their wine with water, the implication seemed to be that their wine was particularly harsh and needed a little chastening. The Italians still add water - *allungato* or *vino battezatto* - if they find the wine is none too smooth. It is said that the French and Italians have always mixed water with their wine. Apparently, this was to avoid the tragedy, recorded by Herodotus, of Cleomenes, a king of Sparta, who having lived among the barbarous Scythians acquired the habit of consuming his wine neat, and thereafter went completely mad!

However, modern research has cast a quite different light on the quality of wine produced during the Roman period. They did in fact mix their wine with water, not because it was too harsh, but because it was too sweet.

Indeed, it may have been close to syrup, a state required to facilitate its movement over great distances as sunken vessels throughout the Mediterranean testify. When the sugar content is raised to over 30% the yeasts cannot convert all the sugar to alcohol, and thus the liquid remain sweet.

How they would have dealt with a local wine that tended towards sweetness, but not classified as such - *abboccato* - is not specifically related.

As Italy has warm, and occasionally extremely hot climatic conditions, such essence would have been unacceptable as a thirst quencher, whereas the addition of water would have reduced it to a palatable level. Add to this the fact that if water itself had to be cleansed of microorganisms then wine was the perfect vehicle for their demise, and not the consumers!

Typhoid germs die swiftly when mixed with wine, being unable to survive and multiply in the tannic and alcoholic medium of wine's acidic pH.

Both the grand Benini wooden casks held some twenty *quintali.* Viticulturists always refer to wine in the cask as so many *quintali,* which is a measurement of weight, not capacity. The word is an adaption of the

Arabic *qintar*. Each *quintale* is reckoned at 100 litres, so it isn't a difficult conversion. Both wooden casks held 2000 litres, (440 imperial gallons).

In some vineyards the *cantine* will still sell their wine by weight, particularly when the purchase is into a demijohn or *damigiana*, which can vary considerably in weight if of the hand-made variety; perhaps by the equivalent of one litre (33.81 fluid ounces). The demijohn is weighed empty and the load marked, then that figure is subtracted from the weight of the bottle when full.

The only British approximation to a liquid weight, in this sense, is the avoirdupois weight, dram, which is one-sixteenth of an ounce or a small draught of spirit. It seems that a Scottish 'wee dram' was very small indeed! The perverse English used the measurement 'quintal' in the fifteenth century, but for 100 pounds, not kilograms. This was a chronic period of deflation, so perhaps it was not surprising.

The white wine of Sant'Anna completed a first fermentation on Guy Fawkes Night, though there were no fireworks to celebrate these two events. Drawn off into a clean vat the residue or solid particles of the wine resembled a pale khaki sludge, quite different in texture from the less solidified *vinaccia* of the red.

All the vats are immediately washed with copious quantities of cold water. This is sufficient for the stainless steel vats, but not the concrete variety. When the latter are dry, a bowl of sulphur is lit and placed inside; the resulting fumes of sulphur dioxide proving an effective disinfectant. The swarms of fruit flies that exit before sealing the pressure plate attest to its efficiency. The sulphur will continue to smoulder inside until the oxygen is used up, and all the bacteria eliminated. Demijohns, and other *cantina* utensils, are also washed in sulphur heavily diluted with water.

Though not directly connected with the finished *sfuso*, when the remaining cake is extracted from the *strettoio* after the first fermentation, and the cloudy liquid, *vino torbo*, (Tuscan dialect) is run off, this not very appealing fluid still has a further use. Unlikely though it sounds, this material could be distilled into a 'house grappa', the strong spirit enjoyed as a *digestivo* throughout Italy.

In times past, and perhaps not so past, copper pot stills could be found among the chicken coups hidden from those official spoil-sports, the financial police. How many secretly remain steaming away, happily converting the discarded waste into something more useful, is not known.

One could make a good case for their 'green' recycling credentials, but naturally, no one does.

As the process was invariably repeated at least twice, and perhaps three times to arrive at a consumable potion, the chickens must have protested, and egg production suffered. Though a proportion of this concoction must have been hooch, not all was a poisonous brew by any means. Many distillers in Tuscany were only too aware of the consequences of irresponsible practices, erring on the side of carefully controlling the purity of the alcohol, and even the flavour. Their family and friends were the consumers, after all.

Some sophistication was achieved by the favourite practice of adding orange peel or herbs to the heated liquid mush, imparting an individual taste to the distillation. Fennel gives the spirit a pronounced taste of aniseed, for example - or so we're told!

Compressed *vinaccia*

We'll continue with a little discourse on the sweeter things in life. To those imagining that the decanting of the *vino fiore* would lead to a peaceful interim while the secondary fermentation blubs and bubbles in splendid isolation, they'd be disappointed. The sorcerers have designs on the natural order of things.

After all, every wine maker intending to produce *sfuso*, no matter how insignificant, and having gone to great pains to arrive at such a point, has aspirations towards everyone being satisfied with their efforts. They may not desire accolades, but compliments never go amiss.

Mostly, the producer will not be a faceless entrepreneur invisible in some far away city, but Luigi from down the road, who wants to look you straight in the eye, not pass by on the other side of the street.

His wine may not be classed as a hyped Super Tuscan, and nothing near, but he wants you to think highly of his *sfuso* even if the distinction rises no higher than a personal verbal acknowledgement '*genuino*', which counts as a truly 'genuine' compliment.

However, one such decision remains to trouble them: whether or not to apply a controversial, and slightly vexed treatment, if the alcoholic strength of the wine is not as it should be. Provocative, in the sense that it is not something that appears readily on the label of a bottle of wine. Nor will you know if such a treatment applies to a particular *sfuso*, but at least you can ask if you're purchasing such wine from a vineyard.

With a commercial product one can assume that the type of grape appears somewhere, the odd 'E number' if the wine's travelled far, and how much brake horsepower they've managed to squeeze out of it.

Ah! Squeezed out of it. Tuned, you mean?

Yes. That's about the gist of it.

You may perhaps recall that wine's alcohol content depends on the natural level of sugar in the grapes. A long, hot summer will ensure very high levels of sugar; and a lack of sufficient sun, just the opposite.

The extraordinary Primitivo grape grown in the Salento peninsula of Apulia, illustrates how much this matters. The name is not a reference to an ancient grape variety, but to the ripening characteristics that allow it to be the first to reach maturity. This argument in respect of the name does not appear particularly plausible, but as so much in southern Italy, its origins appear to be Greek! If one stretches the imagination to consider early man as primitive, that is the first, then it must be possible to consider an early grape as *primitivo*, surely?

This precocity, due to a little natural 'squeezing' from the sun, turns out to be extremely useful if, like Horace, you're a confirmed toper in a hurry.

The Apulian *vendemmia* takes place in mid-summer if they want to keep the alcohol down to about 14°; if not, they harvest the grapes in late summer where it can reach 18°. If they let it shrivel in the sun a little longer they probably produce the strongest naturally dry wine in the world. Technically, they might be classified as fortified wines, those that have a distilled spirit, generally brandy, added at the first fermentation, or at the end of the complete fermentation, depending if a dry or a sweet wine is required. That is not the case with the basic Primitivo wine.

Apulian wine makers have not taken to creating an internationally rated fine wine from the Primitivo grape, though one or two bottles of definite potential have recently been filtering on to supermarket shelves. Historically, little has been produced in that area for ageing in casks.

They have; however, taken advantage of the natural strength of their wine, demonstrated by the huge French registered stainless-steel tankers heading north on the old 'Autostrade del Sole.'

Eventually, Primitivo will lift the alcoholic levels of northern wines by judicious blending. In this respect, one man's loss is another's gain.

Well, what's to be gained, and why?

In most wine producing countries, in poor years additional sugar may be added, a process known as chapatilization. This is not an underhand practice, as some of the great wines of the world are produced in this way. Champagne allows for up to 20 grams of sugar to be added at disgorgement, depending on the preference for brut or demi-sec. The legendary Krug never used to go so far. Favouring a dryer wine, they drew the line at 5-7 grams of sugar.

However, it is something of an art, and the French, having always paid special attention to such matters in the making of wine, leave this critical measurement to the chemist.

To maintain the particular characteristic of a wine the producer may decide it is a smidgen too dry and must be adjusted. This holds true for *sfuso* as well, but the precision is not so critical. The serious producer will study the chemist's results carefully.

The Beaumé Measurement established in the laboratory works out at approximately 1° Baumé equalling 18 grams of sugar in every one litre of wine. As a yardstick, the dissolved solids in grape juice with a rating of 1° Baumé when fermented into a liquid will equal about 1% alcohol. 13°-13.5° Baumé is considered necessary in some quarters to make a good wine. So if you're unlucky to be on a reduced sugar diet, remember Doctor Baumé!

Such manipulation to the organic purist is no more than legal manipulation. In Italy such a practice is controversial, and commercially prohibited. Any correction that has to be made is accomplished by the addition of southern grape varieties, always, as indicated, high in natural sugar. No Tate & Lyle sponsorship here.

But the addition of sugar is not what concerns many commercial wine makers, while the addition of grapes can be a serious embarrassment.

If close to the maximum under consortium rules it will almost certainly alter the character of the wine. To avoid this it is eschewed by the pedantic viticulturist who might well 'illegally' add refined sugar that does not affect the fragrance or the grape. If you have laboured hard to create a style of wine with particular nuances, many would consider this perfectly reasonable, as the results of international competition prove.

That's the contrasting commercial position. Such legal niceties do not necessarily hamper *sfuso*. As much of the wine produced on a small farm is not technically for sale, such a practice is permissible, and as a great many local farmers misguidedly believe that the 'stronger the better' where wine is concerned, sugar will certainly be at hand for any rude adjustments.

The *vino fiore* will have been analysed to see if the fermentation has been adequate. In grapes, natural fermentation theoretically stops at 14° alcohol, though such a figure is somewhat arbitrary and hypothetical. As we have seen, the grape's 'must' in very hot climates is often higher in alcohol where it often exceeds 18° of alcohol by volume, or conversely, in cooler areas, can be enhanced considerably by the *recioto* process.

As alcohol has a subsidiary purpose in maintaining the health of the wine by limiting the risk of infection, Benini likes to ensure a figure as close to 13° as possible. Anything higher merely brings an extra smile to his face.

Nearly all wine has a much slower secondary fermentation that may not be activated immediately, so estimates on how the wine will finally turn out, depend on the experience of the producer. This activity is more critical in the white, which can often remain dormant until the warm air of spring wakes it up.

Benini will only be concerned if the first fermentation proves to have been inadequate, which mostly occurs in a particularly rainy season when the bloom has been diminished on the skin of the grapes. Then a correction has to be made.

Leaving aside the addition of sugar, remember that the approved way of reaching the legally defined *governo* in Tuscany for Chianti was traditionally made by using up to 15% of the liquid from dried grapes or wine 'musts'. This proved hardly practical for very small producers, and so they use the addition of a *mosto concentrato,* a natural augmentation using southern grape 'musts' in a cake form. At Sant'Anna a few cartons of an Apulian variety are purchased as a stand by in case the chemists analysis proves that their grapes have been deficient.

Plus a kilo or two of sugar!

Benini, like many an old hand, has little time for such negative analysis. He only laughs at such misgivings, bursting into a short musical excerpt, such as *'Viva il vino spumeggiante',* one of his frequent operatic arias, treated in a nonchalant cavalier fashion as Turiddu does in the opera 'Cavalleria Rusticana':

(Trans.) Hurrah for the sparkling wine,
Bubbling in the glass
Bringing happiness
Like a lover's smile.
Hurrah for friendly wine
That livens every thought
And banishes melancholy
In cheerful drinking.

Benini believes that the end result is everything, and if it needs a bit of fine-tuning, so be it.

The composer, Mascagni, having been born in Tuscany, has certainly got a lot to answer for - unless the librettists were thinking of champagne, which seems unlikely among Sicilian peasants.

Despite this inconsistency, there is a tradition in the region, and perhaps elsewhere, to have a little of the red wine in December, just prior to Christmas before the second fermentation is complete. It is mostly slightly effervescent, or *frizzante*, indicating it is still working to some degree. Bubbles may not be apparent, but it is certainly prickly on the tongue.

It is something of an Anglo-Saxon prejudice to consider this practice precocious, a belief that it distorts enjoyment of the true character of the wine, which can only be revealed in a given period of time. That's a subjective opinion, of course, as while the wine is active the character is in a constant metamorphosis. Being thus changeable, the optimum point in a wine's life can be as surely missed as it was once remembered. It may be pertinent to say 'it is ready' to drink, or not, but hardly when the optimum point has been reached. And then, when all has been consumed and becomes merely a historical memory, it might be quite difficult to recall that precise point with any accuracy.

I believe everyone must have heard of that mysterious bottle languishing in some dusty corner long past its vintage, that on opening turns out to transcend all previous experience.

One should always, it seems, enjoy wine for the moment. There are only so many dusty corners in a life.

XV: A Question of Taste.

It was a bumper year for wine. Not perhaps of the highest rating throughout Tuscany, but Sant'Anna made 2000 litres of red, and 2500 litres of white wine which, for the Benini family is, by any stretch of the imagination, a great deal of wine.

The red, which had produced a much higher volume of grapes than the white, had returned from its analysis carried out by a laboratory in Bibbona, Tuscany, with a rating that peaked at 12.5° for the red, and 14.0° for the white, with a lower sugar content than the previous year. No doubt this will be put down to the earlier *vendemmia* for like 'sham Abraham' it didn't rain. With more grape sugar from a later start to the *vendemmia* the red might have peaked at 13°, which would have been a very satisfactory figure, and more in line with the normal grade for *sfuso* in the area, but Benini couldn't complain having decided not to risk the onset of poor weather.

The white at 14.0°, when it completed the second fermentation, would suit sleepy summer lunches when the breeze has dropped, leaving the temperature to hover soporifically over 35°C. and the comfort of a hammock is one's only inclination.

For the moment, the *bollitore* were left firmly on the top of the vats, bubbling away happily in the cantina while the wine completed its much longer second fermentation. It would be three months before the musically popping *bollitore* of the red ceases, yet another two more before the white finally gives way to silence.

Because of nature's largesse not all the wine managed to squeeze into the closed vats for the second fermentation. What then was the solution?

Wise to nature's whims, and the possibility of 'the cup running over', a remedy was quick to hand.

Casting your mind back to the old wooden *tino* fondly described by Benini, you'll remember that it had no lid that could be sealed, requiring constant attention to keep the skin and peel down towards the bottom of the vat. He was about to push this method a stage further.

The vats about to be called into service had no lids that could be closed either, but were destined to receive wine that had passed the first fermentation stage. Though free of *buccia*, the liquid still held a quantity of fine debris and yeast in suspension that might pause for a period before it resumed working. Obviously such a condition was not desirable in an unsealed container.

Two open fibreglass vats holding 400 litres apiece, kept for such an emergency, are washed down and set up alongside the other vats. Their strength and suitability cannot be in doubt when you consider that both yacht and automobile bodies employ this material. Having a resin matrix it is also very smooth, sharing much in common with the coating inside a concrete vat. Despite appearing a retrogressive step, the process proved to work remarkably well. Whether they would be suitable for an extended period hasn't been established, as at Sant'Anna, promptly after the second fermentation ceases, they are the first to be decanted into glass demijohns. Though an experiment in itself, Benini is not willing to risk the rewards of a harvest on prolonged experimentation with such containers.

Fibreglass vat.

Once the wine has been transferred to these fibreglass vats, a vaseline oil is poured on to the decanted wine allowing it to float freely on the surface as a seal, excluding any ingress of air. This is really only a mammoth version of the same system that will be used later as a seal in the narrow neck of the demijohns. It might also appear to be 'pouring oil on troubled water.' As oil floats on water, so it does on wine.

Additionally, a very loose fibreglass lid is allowed to float on the top of this oil. As a precaution, many inches have been left between the top of the oil and the rim of the vat to allow for any expansion that might take place. Despite this, for many days the gap between the sides of the vat and its floating lid are kept under attentive observation in case the oil shrinks away exposing the wine. More oil can always be added, but 400 litres of vinegar is not a thing to contemplate with any joy.

However, the system has been developed further by the manufacturers eliminating the use of oil. By adding a pump-up seal fitted to the edge of the lid, and fitting a *bollitore*, a complete pressure system is created.

One other method that is used during the fermentation period, but generally for much smaller quantities of excess wine, is the large demijohn. At Sant' Anna it is always used for the *vino stretto* extracted from the lees of the fermentation.

2

Demijohn with *Bollitore*.

From this point on it was a long wait, punctuated by

the early Christmas sampling of the red, with a few trial samplings of the white. This is not a sign of impatience, but a necessary control as the secondary fermentation in the *cantina* may commence almost at once, or perhaps be delayed into the new-year.

At some time during this second period, the outcome of the year's labour will have reached a discernable character, and on no account must this be missed among the mysterious comings and goings of the wine's development; representing, as it does, a rounded result that Benini could be content with.

By the following February the white in a glass revealed a citron colour, fading to a transparent meniscus with little bouquet if a powerful flavour, being somewhat at odds with the idea of smell having an influence on taste. Fresh and dry, with a crispness that suggested the acidity was working towards a better balance, it still puckered the mouth if an aftertaste was sought. In a five-litre *dami* the colour deepened to amber.

The red, sampled from the fibreglass vat, had begun to lose the raw fruitiness, but remained a confusion of tastes, making it difficult to assess which of the defining characteristics would become prominent. A dark rosé colour suggested too high a percentage of Malvasia and Trebbiano, against which the Sangiovese was struggling to assert itself.

This was a problem Benini had foreseen, but could do little about - a preponderance of white grapes had left too high a percentage of the juice to be accommodated somewhere. It has to be accepted that on a small farm nothing is left to waste, which means everything has to be made to fit in, including excessive grape juice. Though hardly a disaster, a higher percentage of white wine used to make the *podere* generic 'Chianti' was going to make a more than subtle difference to that year's red.

It is worth remembering that *sfuso* is not a 'designer wine', and is not subject to infinite control bent on establishing a 'house' palate. *Sfuso* is more often in the hands of nature than the viticulturist, who may also have been bringing in the corn, or tending to their olives, besides other distractions that come with running a farm. In this manner, every year's wine could be patently different.

By May the red wine from the same vat had become as rounded, and as complete as possible, given the absence of barrel ageing. The Sangiovese remained muted, leaving the wine medium bodied and less tannic than the previous years vintage, something Benini was not altogether displeased with.

Lighter in taste, perhaps a little too thin given the higher percentage of white grapes, the result was still pleasant on the palate with a subtle hint of herbs, peppery even, and if one kept the nose down long enough, conjured up the beginning of a bouquet.

By contrast, the white in June turned out to have a fresh penetrating flavour, tangy and lemony, typifying the taste of a wine that lacks the roundness of time. Nothing mellow, ageing and coordinated it was true, but at the same time emphasising all the brightness of its youth. Mildly tart and crisp, it would nearly all be consumed in the next few months under a hot sun, when vivaciousness is a temperament most appreciated.

In deference to an assumed cosmopolitan taste, Benini recommended standing the white wine for thirty minutes in the refrigerator before being poured into the glass. He prefers it at the natural temperature created by a dark corner with a stone floor, muttering something about the perils of giving a shock to the stomach, as well as the taste. Natural is how country Tuscans seem to like their wine. No ageing, no refrigerator. 'Just as it comes'.

As one never seems to get a headache with *sfuso* that has been well made - it is virtually biological after all - the Benini wine went a long way to affirm the quaffing philosophy of its maker. Not a wine with any pretensions; a wine to adorn with magniloquent sentiments. Made solely, if not exclusively, to drink without ceremony. Like its scores of neighbours such a creation serves nothing more prosaic than to compliment the daily culinary activity that sustains the Tuscan way of family life.

Resisting the disdain of wine writers who generally wax lyrical to the point of the satirical, one always hopes to convince the sceptic that the rustic *sfuso* can boast something of a character, despite the shortness of time in which to develop a distinctive quality.

Though unlikely in the way of vacations that the visitor will have the opportunity to sample a range of these wines from different areas - unless the vacation happens to be in the nature of a tour - then as mentioned in the early chapters, it should still be possible to compare quite a few of those from a limited locality.

Summer is as good a time as any to consider a comparison of the different local wines, for it has probably achieved a reasonable balance for northern tastes by then. This can still be very confusing if you consider that wine from vineyards a kilometre apart can be of a very different character, as indeed can those next door.

You may be confined to a great Tuscan city yet still be able to measure the quality of the local vineyard *sfuso* as all the local *trattorie*, and not a few restaurants, will have their own favourite supplier of table wine.

An important thing to remember is that *sfuso* gets lonely on its own. For in much the same way as any true risotto needs butter as well as company; for *sfuso*, three is most definitely not a crowd. Just you, *sfuso*, and food: the cuisine of the countryside, of the region and the place - essentially provincial, like the wine.

It would be a great disappointment if the traveller didn't remain open minded to the simple integrity, often artless enterprise, of the small farms studding the Italian countryside.

For this reason we can say that *sfuso* is 'honest', not subject to flights of imaginative creation. This is not to say that an aged wine is 'dishonest', of course, providing the adjustments do not adulterate or distort our legitimate expectations of such a wine. Which is not to exclude the possibility that *sfuso*, in company with all wine, doesn't need the benefit of a helping hand.

Unhappily, too much appellation wine has the unfortunate assistance of mechanical and chemical technology, distorting the concept of 'honest'. Very much in the manner of effervescent water, of which there are not so many natural products among the myriad offerings set before us.

Given that *sfuso* is considered a mere bagatelle by the cognoscenti, we can only allow ourselves to judge a wine where the fruit naturally creates a style of its own, regardless whether or not the wine has the potential for fustian observation, or any sort of contrived distinction that sets it apart. Why bother? You are never going to meet it again, for it is not only a wine of the year, but also of any year. There is an absolute immediacy about *sfuso*. Living for the moment.

It can be difficult to enumerate what gives a wine its

identity, for without the 'black arts' of the *oenologist* contriving to replicate a house taste, the wine remains in the 'lap of the gods'. Conditions inside the *cantina* can be controlled, though much hinges on the grape and its quality, something that will vary from year to year, especially if there are a variety of grapes. No one on a small farm has the time to blend one vintage with another to maintain an optimum style. There really is no incentive - which is one of the advantages of not having a name.

Taste, in this case, turns out to be about everything, and nothing. Taste is personal, and subject only to you. With *sfuso* you could concentrate on the fruit by knowing the variety, often Sangiovese, because as the premiere Tuscan grape that is what you can learn to recognize - with perhaps a hint of something else that keeps the wine on your tongue for just a moment or two longer.

It is probably fair to say that a higher percentage of one variety of grape might well disguise the smaller percentage of another; yet the latter may still be adding a great deal to the character. It is not so easy, when you remember you are auditioning that 'cast of thousands'.

There is also, for example, the problem of how to recommend a wine when it isn't likely to be available by the time someone arrives to taste it. With *sfuso* it's an instantaneous matter, not something left until next year. In its own way it's a great deal more difficult than predicting the weather.

One has to learn to enjoy that moment, sometimes memorable, sometimes not - one that will probably never be exactly the same again.

Surprisingly, though there's certainly enough variety to entertain an inquisitive aficionado, at the Tuscan table few locals show a great deal of interest in such pretensions. *Sfuso* compliments country food, and in Tuscany with its rich gamey, salty cuisine, and delicious oily succulence, the wine needs to have grip. It has to have a cutting edge sharp enough to restore the palate to some physiological datum point.

To match a *'Papperdelle di Cinghiale'* to a superlative 1977 Altesino Brunello in the local restaurant would be brutal, like eating corn flakes with champagne. That again is a matter of taste for which, naturally, there is no accounting!

In the way of things, *sfuso* by its very nature will

never need the assistance of those of a mercenary nature where profit is their only business. It has no use for chips of oak added to the fermentation, or thin staves lining an older barrel to eschew the full art of the cooper; the fit not being critical as the barrel still has to be 'wet' to function properly. Say absolutely nothing of micro-oxygenation (small amounts of oxygen pumped through the wine). Nor filtration, which must snatch away the smell and taste trapped in natural deposits, let alone the sugar on which the wine lives. Such techniques only produce a pasticcio resembling the real thing. It may have the reflection, but never the substance.

Sfuso, in any case, remains too humble for such affectation. One might be inclined to say that such authenticity is too transient and austere for the competitive rules of commerce, and thus has no critical approval to add to its value.

In a way that is its true value: an ability not to disturb the extraordinary pleasure of food. You can virtually ignore it because it has cost so little, leaving the wine to replenish the taste buds without searching for those distinctive elegant notes, those harmonious qualities that linger on your tongue long after its statement has vanished. Such a quest is for another occasion, when you are of a different temperament, and not so distracted by appetite!

In this Etruscan heartland they have graciously left it to Horace to offer the alternative inebriate's view:

> Mongst the trees the hallowed grape-vine thou must plant the first of all
> Round the kindly slopes of Tibur, and by old Catilius' wall.
> Varus! all life's ills and sorrows fate doth on the sober lay;
> Nor without the wings of liquor passeth carking cares away.

XVI: Back to the Beginning.

We have finally reached the end of the viticultural year in the life of Sant'Anna. Benini at last has time to rest in his garden under a Persimmon tree, basil leaves rubbed onto arms and ankles - the perfect repellent for mosquitoes and sundry insects. The table has been laid in what can only be described as the un-spoilt and simple Tuscan manner. It is this alfresco ambience that has come to represent the strongest hold on a foreigner's affections. When you combine it with a refined urbane cuisine, and a modern country cook, then you have a gourmand's paradise indeed.

On an immaculate white tablecloth, displaying its exquisite needlework, the contents of the carafes with their deep golden colour and prickly taste, were a perfect foil for a large bowl of spaghetti complemented by its aromatic tomato and basil sauce. There is a crispy green salad too, stroked with wine vinegar then gently tossed in olive oil, sprinkled with chives, and the smallest amount of savory. Conspicuous are the large roundels of dark red mahogany coloured *bresaola* a dry-salted beef, almost hidden under a scattering of fresh wild rocket and crumbling slithers of Parmesan, sumptuously dressed in olive oil, nutmeg, and lemon juice, all to be mopped up with fat loaves of saltless Tuscan bread, best cut and then torn to size. Finally, in the cool larder patiently waiting their turn, plates of dark purple figs, sliced in two, with mascarpone and half a walnut pressed between them! An excellent way to round off supper accompanied with the espresso coffee, and a fantasia of fruit liqueurs.

This is the essence of true Tuscan food. Delicious and simple. Or, if you prefer, deliciously simple. Well, as the Tuscans will always apologize for the 'frugality' of their domestic suppers, it is best not to continue contradicting them.

You will still find Benini as we had originally found him. His life demonstrating a spacious contentment achieved by a balance between his own existence, and that of the world he inhabits. He has never struggled against it, just persuaded its severe, intolerant spirit to give him a little room. He sits, legs stretched out in front, glass in his hand, as though a cardinal's hat really had been placed firmly on his head. Those renaissance

Catholic princes would have recognized him as one of their own.

The vats, it was true, were no longer flush, the Tuscans being, after all, renowned for their spontaneous generosity. But the months of toil had to be quenched, and having been quenched thoughts will turn once more to that cycle of life revolving around Sant'Anna.

He raises his glass in a smiling toast, and joins in the calm and measured conversation of the family where everyone is given their turn. His sentences are loaded with innuendoes: the difficulty in finding the time to spare for the vineyard; if only he had the occasional help of another pair of hands; improvements he could make, we both know, he will never make.

In his heart he is aware that in the future the vineyard will have to take yet another direction, just one more in the many already experienced. Probably in new hands, for it's doubtful of continuing with another generation who have never known it as their childhood home, having made their own lives elsewhere. The old farmhouse, more faithful than many of the human proprietors who have passed through its doors, will find itself ripe for conversion into holiday apartments for those visitors who come seeking the authentic Tuscany during the summer months. Sadly, few will realize it is already slipping into the modern world.

In this, no doubt, the building will find a use more fitting to the present age, though the old chapel will probably survive in its original traditional form, if for no other reason, than custom and curiosity.

Already, just beneath Benini's endlessly jolly countenance, you catch traces of uncertainty, wisps of disillusionment thrust back out of sight - not about what needs to be done, only about how it can be done. He'd thought to sustain Sant'Anna for the future; nurturing a way of life that might live on, only to see it vanishing, even as he keeps it alive.

History might be slipping through his fingers, but ever the optimist while his hearty indomitable spirit exists, he'll still keep a firm grip on the present, along with those things he loves, and finds worthwhile.

Benini is content drawing off from the *cantina* what he needs, when he needs it, a small five litre *dami* of white or red. He is not an abstemious man, but he knows that it is a very long and arduous journey between one year's *vendemmia* and the next. He will be just as well aware that in a farmer's life, time represents a continuum: 'where the end always turns out to be the beginning'.

With luck, he muses; the wine might last until the next vintage is drawn. But then, perhaps not.

When Benini says, "Have some wine", unlike the March Hare in 'Alice in Wonderland', he happily insists on producing an abundant quantity of his *sfuso* to satisfy the deepest needs.

So you don't have the facility of popping down a country lane and bulk buying your wine. Well, if not, you can still indulge in a little speculative daydreaming.

Sfuso may be the wine most likely consumed in an Italian household, but not all families own a vineyard, and thereby hangs a question. How does one, living in an apartment tucked away in an idyllic hill top town with its own *cantina* in the basement, handle such a large volume of wine? To this one question there are many answers, and to avoid Kipling's 'shut eyed sentry' spoiling our reverie, the following is a description of one such possibility. It does not in any way represent the definitive answer. Here's what you need to know, or something like, if you're going to make a job of it.

Wine containers.

For the purpose of this little fantasy we are considering *sfuso* that is sold loose into containers of various sizes in which the wine can be conveniently transported. We are also obtaining it from a farm for the simple reason that is what we prefer. Therefore, it's no good taking along a motley collection of plastic bottles.

One has to approach this with a modicum of serious intent, begging, borrowing, or buying something that at least looks like you have some good intention. Typically, these are the Italian demijohns - those large glass bottles protected by a stuffed wooden or plastic jacket, with a cork stopper. Alternatively, they may be 20 litre carboys of a plastic variety, that being lighter, are more convenient for carrying, but one suspects that the wine should not be left in them for any appreciable time.

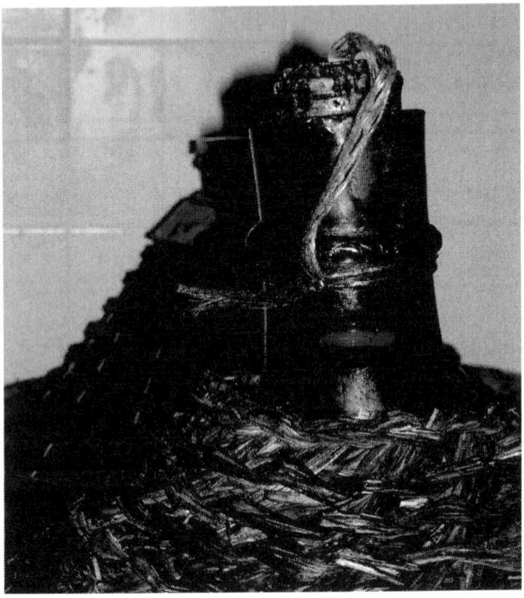

Cork stopper.

The cork cap used in the neck of the demijohn has a small 'V' slit cut on the side to allow for the egress of pressurized gas from within a full bottle. Important for reasons described later. Traditionally, the padding round the glass bottle is hay, freely gathered from the field and dried, but other materials in modern times, such as bubble pack, may have been utilized. A very (very) conservative annual consumption of c.200 litres could be contained in four of these larger vessels holding 54-litres. As one full glass demijohn weighs in at approximately a hundredweight, moving them requires more than one set of strong arms.

Thankfully, they are also available in c.34, 28 and 15 litre sizes for weaker souls - the latter more often being used for the desert wine, Vin Santo, which is nearly always on offer in an Italian home, particularly over Christmas. This may even be obtained as *sfuso* - though I fancy not in a 54- litre demijohn!

In passing, a well-made Vin Santo should not be cloyingly sweet, being very much in the manner of a dry Sercial Madeira. As such it will then be perfect as an English *aperitivo*, as well as an Italian *digestivo*. The commercial varieties are often very luscious, and seldom appreciated by those whose life is spent close to the earth.

Having spent some time in the wood, Vin Santo can't be classified as a 'wine of the year' in the *podere* sense, as three to five years seems the required resting period in wood. There are even stories of it being walled up for decades until an important occasion warrants its removal; generally a matrimony.

A little should now be said about cleaning bottles, and in passing include demijohns, which being second-hand have probably arrived in one's possession in a less than pristine condition. They will need cleansing, no easy task due to the size and shape. The use of detergents or washing up liquids is definitely eschewed for the cleaning of old wine stains that prove particularly stubborn. As commercial cleansing agents have an oily viscosity, even large quantities of water can fail to rid them completely from the glass.

The task can be greatly improved by two methods still commonly practiced. The first is water and fine-grained sand of the sort available from any builder's merchants, though so small a quantity is better begged from a builder. A kilogram of sand, with sufficient water not to negate its abrasive qualities, can be swirled around the stoppered bottle, working it into all the difficult angles. Besides being highly effective, it's also fairly energetic! The second method for a bottle not so heavily stained, uses a too abundant weed - *erba vetriola* - that is best treated with some care, as the leaves, containing sulphurs, can cause an allergic reaction in susceptible persons. In Britain it is known as Wall Pellitory, thriving mostly in central England where, besides the distinction of being either male or female, seems to have no other use whatsoever, except for research into allergies. However as its name suggests - *vetro* being the Italian for glass - in Italy it has a long history of being used for cleaning glass.

A sufficient quantity of the herb, leaves still on the stem, is stuffed into the bottle, filled with water, and left for a day to soften any deposits. Water and herbs are then removed so the bottle can be cleaned with a brush and fresh water. The bottlebrush has a long twisted stem that is flexible, and rotated on the Archimedean principle.

Erba vetriola in bottles.

In either case, the bottles are finally left upside-down to drain and dry completely.

Carboys, now more often in a plastic material, must be washed and dried immediately they are decanted to avoid residual traces of wine etching the material where bacteria can thrive and contaminate any new wine subsequently added. This suggests that decanting should also take place as soon as they arrive in the *cantina*.

Every now and again, the small bottles used to take the wine to the kitchen will need to be cleaned more carefully by being soaked in very hot water with bicarbonate of soda, then rinsed thoroughly.

Having made sure the containers are well washed, and assuming the vineyard is aware of your coming - Luigi will not be amused at being called from his tractor in a far flung field - you can set about realizing the first part of this venture.

The purchasing of *sfuso* can speculatively take place at any time after Christmas while stocks last, but obtaining wine in any quantity is best organized, in the first instance, to coincide with the period when the wine has become a little less lively - approximately in the early spring - and usually ascertained by wine in the glass. At this point, if the wine is a little too lively for your palate, it's best to wait. Giving the wine an extra month won't be looked on eschew by the farmer. For this purpose, most proprietors will probably ask if you'd like an *assaggio*, or a *degustazione* - a tasting - and one has to be bold drinking from a glass that may only be cleansed by rinsing it in wine!

However, as wine is an alcohol and will sterilize the glass, it is best to make use of a custom that will save you a lot of disappointment.

If it's been decided to buy it *fresca*, in the sense of young, perhaps in March, then this makes no difference to what follows, except a sooner return to the vineyard. At this point, the annual custom of purchasing just after Christmas is better left to the knowledgeable.

After the spring it can be purchased at various intervals during the year, though this is not something to rely on, as the vats in a small vineyard are prone to erratic runs on their stock levels. Nor is it desirable to purchase the late vintage, in November or December, unless you have experience of the vineyard, as *sfuso* often displays waning powers. Bottling the whole final purchase at once will mitigate this effect, leaving it to rest soundly for many months. Remember, it's a wine for the year. But, if needs must....

The tasting is necessary, not only for the obvious reason above where you can decide whether the wine is suitable for you, but also because good manners is an aspect of every provincial Italian, and they will certainly notice the absence of it in a guest. Such impressions will go a long way to opening the *cantina* door - and keeping it open.

In the period between *vendemmie,* or vintages, the wine can continue to be active, changing from fresh and sparkling to muscularly mature - 'throwing off' substantial deposits of sugar. It can also become frenetic and *frizzante* if bottled too early and kept too late. At this stage the Italians call the wine *'asprigno'* - rather sharp, prickly and rough - so it's important to know the state of the wine when it's obtained, enabling a decision to be made in the appropriate way.

However, as we're discussing a substantial quantity of wine, one has to be prepared for an occasional noticeable change in quality due to this activity in a still young wine. Not something that happens very often, the natural change being rather too subtle to define.

Hence the argument: if space to store the wine is available purchase a required quantity twice a year, perhaps in May and October, so the quality can be checked again at the second visit. Then, if the taste leaves something to be desired, which would be unusual, there will be the chance of a supporting choice elsewhere. As applicable to most things 'local', there's a good reason for keeping another door open.

Careful assessment of consumption generally dictates how much wine is required. It may be decided that a proportion of domestic wine be purchased at a particular time. For instance, red will be required throughout the year, but white, perhaps, only for the summer months. Unless the vineyard is known to hold sufficient stocks, doing one's sums is an important aspect. By virtue of the demijohn being the same as a vat, there may be nothing lost by purchasing the white with the red in the spring.

To reiterate, late autumn can often be the last chance to obtain red wine from the previous year and may have to last for five or six months over the new year. On the other hand, if a short season for white wine is considered, it means that particular problem doesn't arise; all being consumed by the end of the summer.

In their heyday all *podere* were furnished with a *cantina* on the ground floor, serving to store not only wine, but also provisions needing to be cured or preserved. But it was not a prerequisite of isolated farmsteads alone. Town and village houses had a similar need. One significant feature of *cantina* construction was the absence, or minimizing, of light. Generally, they were quite spacious, and if today they do not need to be so large, they still need to be dark and cool.

Sfuso is definitely not well kept under the stairs, or pushed into the back of the garage, and certainly not neatly stacked in the kitchen or loft. Most of these sites will be too hot, while the garage, perhaps, subject to vibration from father's restored 1930's baby Topolino. All can seriously affect the quality of the wine.

Despite its humble origins, such wine still needs the provision of a sympathetic environment if it is to reach the table in a desirable state.

Out of interest, an Etruscan tomb carved out of the sand varies approximately between 13° and 14°C. or slightly below 58°F. throughout the year. You'll be lucky to have one of those! But there is a disadvantage, as you can't leave precious vintage wines in such an ambience, ideal as they are. The humidity can rise above 80%, at which point the labels may well come off the bottles even if it makes no difference to the wine.

Wine can cope with moderate temperature variations more easily than regular movement, a reason why 'cellarage' in vintners terms means beneath the earth, in a cellar, or vault, where it is dark, cool, and still. Given the weight of a demijohn, domestically, this might not prove very practical. All the same, some effort must be made to maintain an overall cooler ambient temperature for the wine, but also to avoid any movement when decanting takes place. For this reason, the demijohn is often placed immediately on a low platform, slightly above its own height.

For the locals, obtaining these precious vessels is still relatively simple, given that many were produced at the close by town of Certaldo, and have only lately been abandoned as the number of working *podere* diminish. Enquiries among neighbours generally produce a few dusty examples. Jackets for the bottle can still be obtained from agricultural centres both in plastic and wood, though the latter, being made by hand, are considerably more expensive. The choice of having them clad in one material or the other is of some moment, depending on the level of humidity present where they are housed. Generally, those stored above ground can be in wood; those below ground (or in the side of a hill), are more secure in plastic.

At the vineyard *cantina* the demijohn will be filled directly from the vat, or from another demijohn; common just after the *vendemmia*, when space in the vat is needed for the new wine. The wine will have been added just up, and into, the neck of the demijohn, allowing a small quantity of Vaseline oil to form a seal in the narrow aperture. A further 3 - 4 cm gap is advisably left below the cork.

The oil has to be extracted before decanting. If in this process it is not completely removed before the surface area of the wine drops below the neck, it will remain in the wine being decanted into the bottles, finally to reappear floating on the wine in the glass where it is definitely not the place to be. For this reason in the farm *cantina* the vendor will generally bring the wine as high as possible up into the aperture of the narrow neck, and sealed with a minimum of oil. When decanting, the oil can then be removed before you lose sight of it!

Though not in any way imperative if you have confidence in the supplier, they will generally ask if you want a seal? It is perfectly acceptable to negate this procedure at the vineyard, and control the addition of any necessary oil after transit if the intention is to leave the demijohn full for a while. The strait neck will allow little oxidation to take place for a day or two, in much the same way as pulling the cork in a bottle won't allow the wine to breathe sufficiently, given the very small surface area of wine exposed.

Just don't forget!

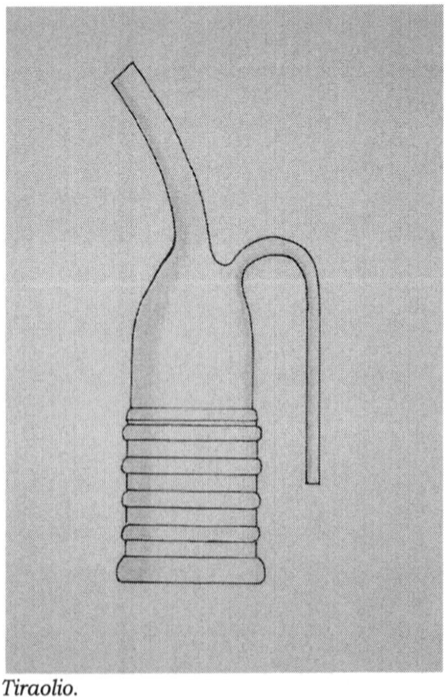

Tiraolio.

Having mentioned the adverse effects of movement, it

follows that if the intention is to decant a demijohn into bottles fairly soon after arrival, then it should be allowed a period of settling down after its journey. This time need not be protracted even if the wine is *'fresca'* or youthful, providing the amount of air remaining in the bottle has been minimized.

If the wine is very young, having for some necessity been purchased a little after Christmas, then it's probably wise to leave it for a period until the New Year has passed. However, there is no hard and fast rule on this, depending solely on the state of the wine.

To remove the oil an appropriately named *tiraolio* is employed. This enclosed plastic bottle has two spouts; the longer passing over the surface of the oil while aspiration is applied to the shorter, lifting the oil off the surface, and into the bottle. The long ends are sometimes extended to accommodate the greater length of neck often found on hand made demijohns. A novice, unaccustomed to the searing quality of atomized alcohol vapour, will initially find the practice accompanied by coughing and spluttering.

Stoppa.

Not being fool proof, a further refinement is provided by turning thick tufts of hemp strands - *stoppa* - across the surface of the wine, effectively soaking up any stray oil that remains there. Decanting can then take place into those small clean bottles.

Bottles to be 'racked', or held in reclaimed table water or beer crates, will not normally be larger than two litres, and more generally of one litre capacity. If the *podere cantina* is conveniently 'next door', then locals will often resort to 5 litre glass bottles, colloquially referred to previously as *'dama'*, from which they pour the wine directly without resorting to any sort of seal. *Sfuso* seems capable of retaining its body for four or five days when kept in a closed container.

One-litre bottles to take metal crown caps - *tappo a corona* - are still available in clear, green or brown glass in the standard Burgundy bottle shape, or more commonly in Tuscany if to take a cork, in a 0.75 cl. Bordeaux style bottle termed *Bordolese*. Two-litre bottles for the crown caps seem no longer to be available in some areas, though the caps are. Bottles with spring lever vitreous caps, and replaceable rubber washers have taken their place. These function adequately if the washers are changed annually. The use of 0.75 cl. standard shape estate bottles can also be recycled by using small cork stoppers - *tappo di sughero* - but are not much in vogue as labels are inconvenient to remove and litre bottles inexpensive.

For some reason it may be found that the two-litre bottles seem to preserve the wine in a better state than the one-litre. No one has a reasonable answer for this - except perhaps your wife - complaining that it gives you a perfectly good excuse for opening a large bottle!

As many months may have passed between the transporting and decanting of wine, the bottles must again be checked for cleanliness. The slightest trace of old wine, even when it has dried out, can spell trouble. A tainted one-litre bottle of wine is just annoying. A tainted 54-litre demijohn is a disaster!

To decant the wine, both in the *podere cantina* and the domestic one, a siphonic system using atmospheric pressure is often employed when transferring from a demijohn. As both the demijohn and the bottle receiving the wine are at atmospheric pressure the demijohn must have its lowest level higher than the receiving bottle. Raising the pressure in the demijohn by blowing down a tube attached to the siphon lifts the wine into a region of low pressure at the top of the tube where it curves and falls into the container, continuing to pull the rest of the wine with it.

Indeed, the domestic implement for this purpose is a little more sophisticated than the length of hose fitted with an extended short piece of split bamboo cane wired to the end used at some vineyards. The domestic version - *gomma del vino* - has all the curves in the right places, plus a tap on the end and an auxiliary aspiratory tube to get the wine started, all housed in a sliding stop so the inserted tube can be held at the right height.

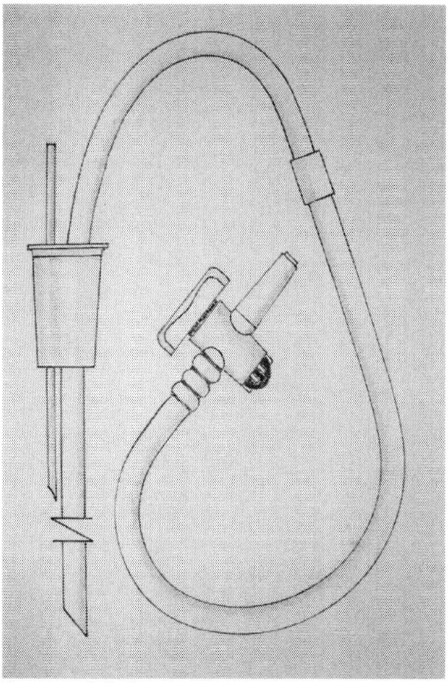

Gomma del vino.

The bottom of the demijohn is convex allowing the tube to stay clear of any deposits that have sunk into the trough at the sides of the base. The shape serves in exactly the same way as the punt in the bottom of a wine bottle. The tube; however, is flexible, and one must often resort to the vineyard *cantina* method of attaching a strip of bamboo against the tube to keep it rigidly perched on the hump, and clear of the silt.

Plastic carboys, not being suitable for lengthy storage, do not have such a facility, and are flat bottomed.

Though deposits in the wine glass are not wanted, their presence in the demijohn is not a bad sign, generally indicating that the wine has been well constructed and might yet have some life left in it.

The process of filling the bottles is straight forward, though two things should be born in mind. One-litre bottles may have very narrow necks, and with the tube inserted there is the possibility of blocking off the egress of air from the bottle as the wine enters. The air is thus forced to escape as backpressure, returning the wine up the tube into the demijohn. It takes a lot of puff to restart a half empty demijohn. A cone shaped funnel with an air vent formed in the side can eliminate the problem.

The other point concerns the amount of wine put into the bottle. In theory it would be useful if the bottles were absolutely full with no empty space, or ullage, at the top; therefore, eliminating the presence of any air. In practice this could turn out to be very unfortunate.

All young wine is cantankerous - at its best when stored free of movement, but in itself never still. As it's often referred to as still 'living' in the bottle, to avoid confusion it might be more realistic to consider the action as 'working'. The presence of deposits (somewhat extreme in vintage port where it is called the crust), is the 'food' the wine continues to feed on. Beside this inherent instability, external conditions can cause quite severe changes in the level of the wine. A protracted period of hot weather may cause a rise in its height, even in a cool cellar. A margin must always be left to absorb this expansion.

Old Tuscans swear by the comings and goings of the moon, and if it can pull oceans there seems little reason to doubt their claim that it can lift wine. A great deal of research has been applied to this phenomenon, and a brief account here may be appropriate to illustrate its effect.

The moon orbits the earth once a month, and the gravitational forces it exerts produces the tides experienced on oceans and seas. This gravitational pull is not equal, exerting as you would expect, a stronger pull on the parts closer to the moon - the spherical form of the earth giving rise to tidal bulges. Nor are the trajectory paths of earth and moon consistent, even if they are constant, expanding and retracting in a given cycle. Therefore, the Harvest Moon is the full moon closest to the Equinox - a time when the sun crosses the equator resulting in day and night being equal. (Twice a year,

20/21st. March and 22/23rd. September, known as the Vernal and Autumnal Equinox.) Though, so far, there appears to be no scientific evidence that such a phenomena directly effects wine, there has been enough empirical evidence to suggest that it does. It is all a question of accepting thousands of years of tradition?

Certainly, the old farmers in Italy didn't risk harvesting, or barrelling, on any day other than those during a waning moon, convinced the wine would be ruined. This belief is stretched to the aberration every four years when the full moon can be as late as the 7th October, though the effects are greater in the northern hemisphere. The falling moon after a full moon is referred to as *'luna calante'*. Whether it is the effect of the moon, or the temperature, the sediment (lees - deposits) will be disturbed, and though an essential asset in wine, should not arrive in the glass. This being the case, the opinion of some experts that the wine will have a different taste in respect to the waxing and waning of the moon has some relevance.

Be that as it may, the level of the wine is extremely erratic. Too full a bottle will apply enormous pressure to the top if conditions alter adversely, capable of cracking or snapping the glass. Even in the demijohn, if the wine rises too far, the oil seal can be dispersed through the pressure slot in the cork top, thus exposing the contents to the air.

Schiuma.

As the wine rushes into the bottle during decanting a considerable quantity of *spuma*, or *schiuma*, is created. This foam contains a fair amount of air, and though quickly subsiding a little ring of bubbles often remains on the surface. These may take some while to disperse, but until they have, the capping is best delayed for some hours.

Advisedly, holding fast to tradition, decant the wine during a waning moon, and leave a reasonable amount of space under the cap.

A fascinating little Tuscan annual in booklet form called 'Sesto Cajo Baccelli', or just 'Baccelli', is an informative agricultural guide describing the monthly activities. Inside you can find all the phases of the moon prominently displayed to assist this essential decision.

During the summer, if by any chance the decanting process is suspended at the point where the wine is in the bottle, but not yet capped, the heady scent can prove to be a magnet for fruit flies who seem to have a suicidal mentality by ending up quite drunk in the neck of any open bottle. Sharing 60% of the human genes, and one very distinct proclivity, this is hardly surprising. Probably the easiest way to protect the wine from any insects is to temporarily cover the tops with small reusable plastic cups.

The preferred way to permanently seal the bottle until needed is by the use of the metal corona cap or *tappo a corona,* similarly found on beer bottles. For this purpose the *tappatrice,* a small press that crimps the metal cap on wine bottles can be used. It is normally supplied with a changeable head attached to a sliding bracket for height adjustments, enabling miscellaneous sizes to be accommodated. If possible it should be clamped to a flat surface as the process can be a little unstable if reasonable care is not taken.

Once this has been completed, the full bottles of wine can be safely stored in the coolness of the *cantina.* With metal caps you can leave the bottle in a vertical position as there is nothing to be gained in laying them down. Indeed, even if they had corks, it is highly unlikely that shrinkage would be a problem in so short a period before consumption.

That should keep you busy while keeping in mind the Tuscan proverb: Buy your wine, and your wife, nearby.

So, as you reach for the bottle opener, consider: that if on occasion you're lucky enough to be able to enjoy the nectar like quality of a wine approaching that of a 1977 Altesino Brunello Riserva - remember that this excellent and superlative Brunello, but for the grace of God, (and Giulio Consonno) could have been just a humble sfuso.

(Note: Until 2002, when it passed into other hands, the proprietor of Altesino was the Milanese business man, Giulio Consonno, who, at the same time as rearing some of the finest Arab horses in Italy, ran the estate with his manager C. Basla and enologist P. Rivella.)

Photo endnotes:

Bigoncia and *Frollatura.*

The *bigoncia* was a medieaval chest used for carrying grapes, and is first mentioned in 1321. It was used until plastic crates became available. The size is measured in litres, c.150.
The *bigoncio* was very similar in appearance, but wider and lower. Often fitted with handles, making it suitable for carrying grape juice and other liquids.

The paddle standing next to it is a *frollatura* described with its use on p112 of the text.

Vineyard battalions.

Buying direct!

The Novice's Lament

You have enlightened me much
But you have taught me little,
Much of what you do
But little of what you know,
You have shown me how
But not the instinct that tells you when,
Time has not been the same for us
Nor the same for other men.

GLOSSARY
APPENDIX
FURTHER READING
INDEX
NOTE PAGE

Glossary - Italian words and phrases used in text.

a tavola	to the table.
abboccato	wine tending to sweetness.
aceto	vinegar.
acetobacter	vinegar bacteria.
affettati misti	a plate of sliced, cured meat.
All'arrabbiata	pasta with piquante tomato sauce.
allungato	wine with water added.
amaro	bitter taste.
aperitivo	pre-dinner drink.
aratura meccanica dei filare	hand held machine for weeding.
arricciamento delle foglie	the leading shoot.
asprigno	sour taste.
assaggio	a tasting
azienda agricola	farm.
baccelli	broad beans picked from the pod.
barba	beard
barbatelle	rooted cuttings.
benissimo	very well, in sense of excellent.
bocciodromo	bowling pitch.
bollire	to boil.
bollitore	pressure valve on vat.
bosco	woods.
botte	barrel or cask.
bresaola	dry-salted beef.
buccia	peel or skin of grape.
buono	good.
calanchi	geological volcanic gullies. Volterra.
cambretta	steel staple.
cameratismo	comradeship.
campagna	the country, in sense of farmland.
canniccio	a cane mat.
canti estemporanei	a lengthy ballad or verse.
cantina(e)	cellars or wine vaults.
cantuccini	Prato: a hard biscuit with almonds.
carbonaie	storage place for carbon.
carbonari	charcoal makers.
carroccio	a mobile altar.
cartoccio	spade with curling shaped blade.
casalingo	homemade .
cena	supper.
cesto di vimini	a wicker basket for grapes.
Cinta Senese	Siena: pigs that forage freely.
ciocca	lock of hair.
cirro	curly tendril.
comune	town/city council.
comune sfuso	a local wine.
concime	manure.
consorzio	association or society.

contadino (a)	farmer/male (female)
cordone orizzontale	single stem of an espalier.
corretto	a correction to alcohol grade.
crostata	jam tart.
DOC	Denominazione di Origine Controllata.
DOCG	D:O:C Guarantita (Italian wine laws).
dama	(colloq) a squat five litre bottle.
damigiana (e)	demijohn.
degustazione	a tasting.
digestivo	after dinner drink.
diraspare	picking grapes from the bunch.
diraspatrice	machine for stripping grapes off stalk.
enologo (i)	wine maker (s)/chemist (s).
enoteche	wine shop/vintner.
erba vetriola	the herb wall pellitory.
etto	100 grams.
Fagioli con Salsicce	recipe for white beans and sausages.
fattoria	Villa-estate farm.
fave (a)	broad beans.
favetta	small broad beans.
femminelle	stems not bearing fruit.
festa	feast day/celebration.
fiaschi	wine bottle, often covered in straw.
Finocchiona	a salami with fennel.
Fiorentina	a type of salami.
Focaccia	a type of bread, originally Ligurian.
frollatura	a wooden impeller used in old vats.
frangizolle	disc harrow.
frantoio	commercial oil press/mill.
fresca	fresh wine, just drawn.
frizzante	effervescent.
gamberetto	shrimp or prawn.
gambero	crayfish.
gambretta	staple (colloq).
gastronomia	food department-delicatesen.
genuino	genuine, in the sense of honest.
ghiaioso rosso	red gravel
gomma del vino	wine siphon.
Governo alla Toscano	legal definition of added alcohol.
Grandone	nickname expressing size or strength.
grappolo	a bunch (of grapes).
graticci	type of cane mat (colloq).
il vino locale	local wine.
insalatina di campo	a countryside salad.
'la vite piange'	sap from a cut vine.
lavorato	'worked' in relation to wine.
luna calante	falling moon after full moon.

madonne	romantic allusion to young ladies.
madre del vino	vinegar bacteria.
malolattica	active fermentation.
margotta	reproduction of plant by layering.
Mascarpone	a clotted cream cheese
metabisolfito	chemical used in vineyard.
mosto concentrato	a strong 'must' of grape sugars.
muffa grigia	grey mould.
occhi	eyes in reference to grape shoots.
orrendo	horrible.
osterie	rustic restaurants or inns.
padrone	master.
palo (i)	pole/post.
pappardelle	long, flat, crinkle edged pasta.
Pappardelle di cinghiale	pasta with wild boar sauce.
pasto di mezzogiorno	midday meal.
pastori (e)	shepherds.
per favore (piacere)	please.
perenospora della vite	mildew.
piazza (e)	town square.
pici	type of pasta.
pigiadiraspatrice	removing grapes from the stalk.
podere	farm.
Polpette alla pizzaiola	rissole with anchovies and mozzarella.
pranzo	lunch.
Primitivo	grape variety, and wine of that name
primo palo	first post.
propaggine	reproduction of plant by layering.
quintali (e)	a weight (two hundred weight).
Radicchio rosso	a type of chicory, red in colour.
ragù	minced-meat sauce.
raspi (o)	grape stalks.
razzole	the cut branch.
recia	ear (colloq).
recioto	production of a strong grape must.
reginelle (regnette)	a type of pasta.
riccio	curly.
Riforma Agraria	agricultural reform.
Riserva	term implying superior quality wine.
rustico	rustic, rural.
sacerdote	priest.
salsicce di cinghiale	wild boar sausages.
salume	various pork products.
sasso di terreno	preparation of the soil.
sbarbettatura	pruning of fine roots.

sbriciolona	a type of pork salami.
scarola	a type of lettuce.
schiuma	see spuma.
soppressata	pressed boiled meats.
spedaletto	small hospital.
spuma	air bubbles on top of wine.
stoppa	hemp strands for removing oil traces.
stranieri (e)	foreigners.
strettoio	machine for pressing grape 'must'.
'troppe foglie'	too many leaves.
tappatrice	a small crimping press for metal caps.
Tappino	nickname expressing small.
tappo a corona	metal bottle top.
tappo di sughero	cork for sealing bottle.
terrae filius	son of the soil.
testucchi/testucchio	Etruscan : very small trees.
tino	a large wooden vat.
tiraolio	a plastic bottle for removing oil.
torchio	wine press.
torculum	wine press.
torta	jam tart.
tralcio	young branches.
trattoria	rustic restaurant.
trivella	two handed auger.
tumultuoso	agitated.
vangheggia	tool for loosening buried rocks.
vendemmia	wine harvest.
Vernaccia	grape variety and name of wine.
vestiti	demijohn jackets.
vetro	glass.
vigneto	vineyard.
villa fattoria	villa with large estate.
vin cotto	heated wine.
vinaccia	grape skins, seeds etc.
vino battezzato	wine and water.
vino della casa	the house wine.
vino della tavola	table wine.
vino fiore	wine from the first fermentation.
vino locale	local wine.
vino stretto	pressed grape liquid. (see Strettoio)
vino torbo	unclear wine, agitated, turbid (colloq).
viti selvatiche	wild grapes.
vitici	grape tendrils.
zappa	adze like gardening tool.

Appendix.

Numbers as Names. Endings in 'o', are masculine

1. Primo; - Primella; Primetta
2. Secondino; - Secondina
3. Terzilio; - Terzilia
4. Quartilio; - Quartilia
5. Quintilio; - Quintilia
6. Sestilio; - Sestilia; Sestina
7. Settimo; - Settima
8. Ottavio; Ottavino; - Ottavia; Ottavina
9. Novelo; - Novela
10. Decimo; - Decima
11. Ultimo; - Ultima; Finimola

The seven defined zones for Chianti are:

Classico
Colle Aretini
Colli Fiorentini
Colline Pisane
Colli Senesi
Montalbano
Rùfina

This in no way indicates that the wines will be superior, only that they will have been produced under consortium rules.

Size of vats mentioned in Chapter XIII

The liquid capacity of the vats is confusing if not in litres. The British Imperial gallon is 4.546 litres and the American gallon is a smaller 3.785 litres.

Hampton Court

A royal palace of Henry the Eighth, built in the London Borough of Richmond upon Thames. The 'Great Vine' is open to the public, and is best seen after the August Bank Holiday. The grapes can be purchased during the first three weeks of September.

Soppressata

The original is a highly flavoured pork and beef salami from Verona, Padua, and Venice. Other regions have their own variation of pressed meat. The Roman version was said to be just a pig's head including figs and honey. *Coppa*, which is similar, is made from a shoulder of pork.

Further Reading - a personal guide.

There are very few books on table wine classified as *sfuso*. The following provide a helpful background.

'Folklore by the Fireside'. Alessandro Falassi. Scolar Press 1980.

'Vino'. Burton Anderson. Little, Brown and Co. 1980.

'The Origin and Ancient History of Wine'. McGovern, Fleming and Katz. Gordon and Breach 2000.

'Compendio Enologico'. Professor Tullio de Rosa. Edizione Librex 1969.

'Roman Antiquities: Manners and Customs of the Romans'. Alexander Adam 1822.

The works by Falassi and de Rosa will be of immediate interest in conjunction with 'Loose Wine' though I'm not convinced de Rosa is available in English. Despite that, the photographs are worth your while seeking it out.

Though not about *sfuso*, Burton Anderson's pocket guide to Italian wines, published by Mitchell Beazley, accompanied me all over Italy in the eighties and nineties. They are still available, and indispensible. His very informative book 'Vino', on Italian wine, remains a classic.

That by McGovern *et al.* is a book for serious students of the prehistoric and ancient origins of wine. Particularly instructive on botanical issues.

Adam was very knowledgeable on all aspects of Roman life, and the section on agriculture answers not a few questions on the growing of vines. Very obscure, and probably difficult to obtain now outside antiquarian bookshops.

INDEX

Abboccato. 114
Abruzzo - wine from. 80
Acetobacter - bacteria. 106
Adjustment - of wine. 119
Advocaat. 114
Adze - *zappa*. 56
Agricultural - practice. 54
Alice in Wonderland. 132
Allegrini - Amarone. 77
Allungato. 114
Altesino - Brunello. 128,147
Amarone - *sfuso*. 78
Amarone wine - scent of. 77
Amphion. 12
Anderson. Burton. 9
Anglo Saxon. 19
Apennines. 28
Appelation wine. 127
Apulia. 14
Apulian musts. 120
Apulian vendemmia. 118
Arbour. - for vines. 48
Archimedean Screw. 46
Asprigno - wine. 138
Axe-adze - Roman. 56
Azienda Agricola. 28,54
Baccelli . annual. 146
Bacci.Nilo. 7,86,99
Bacon. Sir Francis. 13
Bamboo. 43
Barbatelle - cuttings. 46
Barbera - grape. 80,81,111
Barrels - cost of. 109,110
Barrique. 18
Basket weavers. 48
Bath. 31,41
Baxandall. Prof. Michael. 53
Beans - fertilizer. 34
Beaujolais Nouveau. 20
Beaumé measurement. 119
Benini - and buds. 59
Benini - and casks. 114
Benini - and sugar. 120
Benini - the future. 130
Benini. Lorenzo. 3,5,6
Benini *passim*:7,12,17,23,24,25,26, 27,28,30,31,33,34,35,36,38, 55,57,60,61,62,67,69,79,80, 82,84,90,99,122
Bibbona - laboratory. 122
Blake.William. 32
Blanc de Valdignes. 50
Bocciodromo - bowling. 26
Bollitore. 99,105
Bordolese - bottle. 142
Botte. 113
Botticelli - Volterra. 53
Bottles - cleaning. 135
Bottles - sizes of. 142
Branches. 59
Bristol - shipping. 31
Broad beans. - 58
Brunello - clone. 80
Brunello di Montalcino. 18
Brunellogate. 18
Brussels - bureaucrats. 38
Brussels. 9
Buccia. 112,122
Buds. 59
Burgundian. 2
Burgundy - bottle. 142
Burgundy. 111
Buying wine - by weight. 115
Cabernet - as correction. 77
Cambretta . staples. 44
Canniccio - mats. 76
Canti Estemporanei. 7
Cantina - type of. 133,138
Cantina - vendemmia. 85
Capping - bottle. 142
Carbon dioxide. 103
Carbonaie. 55
Carboys. 134
Carmingnano - Redi. 71
Cartoccio- spade. 44
Carvel. 15
Casks - marking. 113
Casks. 12
Castro. Fidel. 21
Caterpillar tractor. 39
Cato - De Agri Cultura. 51
Cato. 81
Cecina. 73
Celts. - and augers. 46
Celts. 14
Cement vats. 16
Ceramic vessels. 13
Ceres. 27
Certaldo. 139
Cesto di vimini. 88
Champagne. 118
Chapatilization. 118
Chard - wild. 56
Château Margaux. 11
Chestnut. 14
Chianti - alcohol. 76
Chianti - Colli Senesi. 71

Chianti - Colline Pisane. 71
Chianti - Florence Red. 73
Chianti - regulations. 75
Chianti - zone. 75
Chianti Classico. 74,81
Cholesterol. 35
Cinta-Senese - pigs. 54
Clay - characteristics. 33
Clinker - planks. 15
Co-operative outlets. 22
Colorino.71
Colour - skin. 103
Comune sfuso. 20
Concrete stakes. 45
Concrete vats. 99,108,109
Consortium - Chianti. 74
Containers - for wine. 133
Coopers - adze. 56
Copper stills. 115
Corks - demijohn. 134
Correction. 76,77,120
*Corretto.*82
Cossa. F. della. 56
Cretan - adze. 56
Crus. 11
DOC 10,11,24
DOCG 10,11,24
Dame Jeanne. 108
Dami. 125
David. Elizabeth. 95
Decanting - process. 141
December - tasting. 121
Demeter. 27
Demijohn - filling of. 139
Demijohn - source of. 108
Demijohn - weight. 134
Demijohn. 107
Deposits - in bottle. 143
Diraspatrice. 91
Domitian. - laws. 37,38
Donizetti. 5
Doves. 58
Dr Dulcamara. 5
Dram. 115
Drinks - mixing. 71
E.U. Cap reforms. 37
Edwardian gardeners. 35
Egg yolks. 113
Egypt - roses. 64
Egypt. 32
Elba. 32
Elysium. 22
Enoteche. 5
Environment. 27
Enzymes. 105
Erba Vitriola. 135
Estate *sfuso.* 73,79
Estate wine. 89
Etruscan - mines. 32
Etruscan. - and augers. 47
Etruscan. - and vines. 47,48
Etruscan. - vine training. 48
Etruscans. 14.
European Community. 36
Fagioli in Fiasco. 34
Fattoria, 28,54
Feeder roots. 57
Femminelle - barren stem. 66
Fennel - grappa. 116
Fermentation - must. 102
Fermentation - complete. 106
Fermentation - initial. 105
Fermentation - second. 122
Fermentation - stopped 105
Fermentation - yeast. 102
Fermentation process. 105
Fertilizer. 57
Fiat bulldozer.
Fibre glass vats. 123
Flanders - winters. 26
Florence Red - dry wine. 73
Florio - farm dog. 104
Frollatura. 112
France. 38
French tankers. 118
French. 18,20
Fresca - young wine. 137
Freud. Sir Clement. 20
Frizzante - wine. 138
Frosts. 26
Funnel - decanting. 144
Gamay Noir. 20
Garlic - wild. 56
Gentile - clone. 80
Ghiaioso Rosso. 32
Gioli. Francesco. 83
Gomma del Vino. 143
Governo alla Toscana. 76
Grand crus. 2
Grandone - nickname. 7
Grape Juice. 102
Grape must. 119
Grape picking - modern. 89
Grape Torniquet. 91
Grapes - correction. 79
Grapes - pressing. 73
Grapes - promiscuous. 84
Grapes - sampling. 85
Grapes - treading. 91
Grapes - weight. 102
Grapes - picking. 87
Grappa - quality of. 116
Grappa. 115
Graves. Robert. 61

Grecale. 25,31,60
Greco-Egyptian. 14
Greek - and fertilizer. 58
Greek heroes. 35
Guidi. 30
Guzzoli.Benozzo - artist. 91
Hampton Court - vine. 68
Hardy rod. 21
Harrow - use of. 40,55
Health of wine. 120
Heracles- 61
Herodotus - Cleomenes. 114
Holes. - digging of. 43
Homer - Odyssey. 78
Homer. - and vines. 49
Hooped barrels. 14
Horace. 15,72,113
Horizontal Cordon. 52
House palate. 125
Humphry Clinker. 66
Italy - and sugar. 119
Jesus. 15
Judaea. 15
Kipling. 133
Krug - and style. 118
La Scala. 3
Land Rover. 31
Languedoc. 11
Lansdown. 31
Latifundium. 28
Lavorato. 18
Layering. 51
Libeccio. 31
Ligurian. 31
Loggioniste. 3
Lombards. 28
Luna Calante. 145
Lupin seeds. 35
Lupins. 34
Macaulay - Lays. 101
Macchiaoli - artists. 83
Madre del Vino. 106
Mahomet. 15
Malvasia. 69
Maremma. 7
Marsala. 81
Mascagni. 121
Masi - Amarone. 77
Mayani. Zacharie. 49
Medici. 30
Mediterranean diet. 19
Mediterranean. 31
Merlot - as correction. 77
Metabisofito. 105
Mezzadria - contract. 28
Mildew. 63
Milk - mildew. 63
Maestrale. 31
Montalcino. 18
Montepulciano. 76
Montescudaio - *consorzio*. 73
Moon - and decanting. 144
Morton.H.V. 1
Mould - treatment. 62,63
Must - boiling of. 15
Must. 77
Names - as numbers. 43
Natural propagation. 51
Nebbiolo. 50,111
New Forest - verderers. 54
Nilo. 7
Nipatella. 6
Oenologist - taste.128
Oenologist. 78
Oil seal - wine. 140
Olive groves - devastated. 26
Olive harvest. 25
Olive oil - per tree. 72
Opimius. 15
Orange peel - grappa. 116
Organic fertilizer. 57
Organic. 10
Orwellian. 38
Oxen - ploughing. 41
Pali. - cross poles. 47
Palio - Siena. 41
Paragon. 31
Pasta - not noodles. 97
Pastori. 55
Pecorino cheese. 38
Persephone. 27
Persia - clay jars. 14
Pheasants - and grapes. 68
Phylloxera Vastatrix. 50
Piccolomini. 30
Piozzi.Mrs. 49
Pitch. 13
Plasic crates. 87,88
Pliny - boiled wine. 81
Pliny the Elder. 15
Pliny. - and augers. 46
Pliny. - and recioto. 79
Ploughing - winter. 55
Po River. 30
Podere - and correction. 79
Podere - vendemmia 84
Podere - wine. 75
Podere Sant'Anna. 25
Podere wine - alcohol. 76
Podere. 12,25,54,74,76 et al
Pomerol. 11
Ponente. 31
Populonia. 32
Portland Cement Vats .12

Portugal .50
Pranzo - description. 94
Pranzo - Roman. 93
Price competition. 89
Primitivo - and name. 118
Primitivo - strength. 118
Primitivo grape. 117
Propogation - grafting. 62
Propogation. - methods of. 47
Prosecco. 71
Provence. 11
Prugnolo - clone. 80
Pruning. 59
Recioto - derivation. 78
Recioto - process. 77
Recioto della Valpolicella. 77
Riforma Agraria. 28
Resinated. 13
Retsina. 13
Ricasoli. Baron Bettino. 74
Riserva. 9,10
Roman - and fertilizer. 58
Roman - torculum. 92
Roman - vineyards. 31
Roman. 14,15
Roman - and squares. 48
Romans. - vine training. 34,41,42,48
Root - regression. 61
Roses - vineyard. 63
Roses - mould. 63
Roses - whitefly. 64
Salento - Apulia. 117
Sand. 33
Sangiovese - correction. 74
Sangiovese - flavour. 111
Sangiovese - taste. 128
Sangiovese - disease. 51
Sangiovese. 74
Sangiovese. 75
Sangiovese. 80
Sangiovese. 37,51,128, passim.
Sant'Anna - and lunch. 92,94
Sant'Anna - chapel. 30
Sant'Anna - Chianti. 73
Sant'Anna - harvest. 66
Sant'Anna - the future. 130
Sant'Anna - vendemmia. 84
Sant'Anna - orientation. 39
Sant'Anna - planting. 50
Sant'Anna. 27,29,31,33,36, 50,51,54,62,69,72,75,80,82, 102,115,124,130
Sap - and taste. 66
Saracini. Torre. 30
Sardinian - shepherds. 38
Sassicaia. 11
Sbarbettatura. 57
Scasso del terreno. 40
Scirocco. 25
Sea water. 13
Second fermentation. 125
Second World War. 28
Sercial Madeira. 135
Shakespeare - Orlando. 93
Sharecropping. 29
Shipwright - adze. 56
Shoots - configuration. 65
Shoots - control of. 66
Shoots - new. 52
Siberian. 31
Silbury. 41
Siphonic system. 142
Slater - hot houses. 50
Smith.Adam. 37,38
Smollet - Livorno. 66
Soil - working. 40
Sotheby's. 12
Spedaletto - and Medici. 53
Spuma. 146
Spumante. 71
St. Luke - opinion. 111
St.Lino - Volterra. 111
St.Peter - Volterra. 111
Stainless steel tanks. 109
Stainless steel vats. 108
Stake - *Primo palo.* 42
Stake - *Ultimo palo.* 43
Standard beverage. 19
Stock - cuttings. 51
Stock levels. 137
Stone's Ginger Wine. 19
Stoppa. 141
Strabo. 109
Strettoio. 107
Strimmer. 56
Sugar. 117
Sulla. 34
Super Tuscans - hype. 117
Super Tuscans. 11
Surveyors. Roman. 41
Sweet wine - Roman. 114
Syrian. 13
Tapatrice. 146
Tappino - nickname. 7
Tappo. 146
Tar Macadam. 32
Technology. 10
Temperature control. 104
Terrae Filius. 8
Tertiary Period. 33
Testucci. - small trees. 48
The Vineyards - Bath. 31

Tino. 112,122
Tiraolio. 141
Torchio. 92
Tramontana. 31
Transporting wine. 13
Trattoria. 2
Treading troughs. 91
Trebbiano. 74
Trivella. - auger. 46
Trombetta da Morto. 6
Tucker.E. 50
Tuscan - cultivation. 36
Tuscan character. 21
Tuscans. 26
Ullage. 109,144
United Kingdom. 20
United States. 29,50,51
Val d'Era. 73
Valpolicella - grape. 77
Vangheggia. - crow-bar. 44
Vasari. Giorgio. 53
Vaseline oil. 123
Vats - cleaning. 115
Veii - Etruscan. 72
Vendemmia - and novice. 90
Vendemmia - and sfuso. 74
Vendemmia - correction. 78
Vendemmia - date for. 84
Vendemmia - festa. 93
Vendemmia - tasks. 86
Vendemmia. 3,17,76,79,122
Vendemmie - as festival. 82
Venosa. 14
Vermiglio. 74
Vernaccia - grape. 107
Vernaccia. 74
Verona. 77
Vin Cotto. 81
Vin Ordinaire. 11
Vin Santo. 135
Vinaccia - skin etc. 106
Vine - growth. 52
Vines. - height of. 45
Vineyard - growth in. 67
Vineyard. - layout. 39
Vineyard. Pompei. 41
Vinification. 20
Vino da Tavola. 3,11,22
Vino della Casa. 3
Vino Fiore. 106,112,117
Vino Locale. 3
Vino Stretto. 107,124
Vino Turbo. 115
Vintage - all wine. 108
Vintage. 11
Virgil. - Georgics. 49
Viticulture. - and cats. 27
Volterra - and olives. 72
Volterra - and vines. 72
Volterra - terrain. 73
Volterra. 71
Water - unreliable. 16
Water Board. 33
Weeds - invasion of. 55
White grapes - mutation. 70
Wicker baskets. 88
Willow - uses. 47
Wind - destruction by. 68
Wine - 'still living'. 144
Wine - change in. 138
Wine - purchasing. 137
Wine - testing. 125
Wine - young. 112
Wine and water. 114
Wood - casks. 18
Wood - oak taste. 110
Wood burning. 35
Wooden barrels. 16,109,110
Wooden casks. 108
Yeast - ambient. 103
Yeast - growth. 104
Yoxall H.W. 111
Zeno - philosopher. 58
Zeno - stoic. 34

J:C:Mack was born in Cornwall, and after a short medley of interests, settled for being a schoolmaster. After a long English residence in Salisbury and Bath, he and his wife are now based in Tuscany. They have one daughter.

NOTES

12259633R00104

Printed in Great Britain
by Amazon.co.uk, Ltd.,
Marston Gate.